THE
POCKET
IDIOT'S
GUIDE™ TO

Spanish

by Gail Stein

alpha
books

A Division of Macmillan General Reference
A Pearson Education Macmillan Company
1633 Broadway, New York, NY 10019-6785

©1999 Gail Stein

Macmillan Publishing books may be purchased for business or sales promotional use. For information please write: Special Markets Department, Macmillan Publishing USA, 1633 Broadway, New York, NY, 10019.

THE POCKET IDIOT'S GUIDE name and design are trademarks of Macmillan, Inc.

International Standard Book Number: 0-02862703-2
Library of Congress Catalog Card Number: 99-60218

2000 99   8 7 6 5 4 3 2 1

Interpretation of the printing code: the rightmost number of the first series of numbers is the year of the book's printing; the rightmost number of the second series of numbers is the number of the book's printing. For example, a printing code of 99-1 shows that the first printing occurred in 1999.

Printed in the United States of America

Publisher: Kathy Nebenhaus
Editorial Director: Gary M. Krebs
Managing Editor: Bob Shuman
Marketing Brand Manager: Felice Primeau
Editor: Jessica Faust
Development Editors: Phil Kitchel, Amy Zavatto
Assistant Editor: Georgette Blan
Production Editor: Stephanie Mohler
Copy Editor: Amy Bezek-Lepore
Cover Designer: Mike Freeland
Photo Editor: Richard H. Fox
Illustrator: Jody P. Schaeffer
Designer: Scott Cook and Amy Adams of Design Lab
Indexer: John Jefferson
Production Team: Marie Kristine P. Leonardo, Angel Perez

Contents

Introduction

Your travel plans include a visit to a Spanish-speaking country or two. Or business opportunities beckon and abound in a Spanish-speaking land. Or your love of languages is driving you to continue your studies. Whether you're traveling, working, or just a student at heart, you want to brush up on your Spanish and you want to do it *now*. Or perhaps you've never studied the language and you need an intensive crash course.

Take a long, hard look around you—Spanish is everywhere. There's no time like the present to familiarize yourself with words, phrases, and expressions that can come in handy on a daily basis. In no time flat, you'll appreciate the advantages that a knowledge of Spanish can bring you, no matter what the situation.

Don't be afraid to dive right in. Do it now! Time is of the essence. If you're looking for a fast yet simple and uncomplicated way to learn to communicate in Spanish, this book will help you master the sounds and syntax of the language with maximum speed and efficiency and with minimum sweat and exertion. You have my promise that learning Spanish won't be a chore. On the contrary, it will be an enriching experience with unforeseen, pleasant rewards.

What's on the Inside

So you want to speak Spanish. Is it because a sexy, Latino accent makes your heart skip a beat and your legs start to wobble? Perhaps it's because the aroma of fine, home-cooked paella makes your stomach growl in eager anticipation of an extraordinary repast. Or is it because seductive ads containing the beautiful white sands and blue waters of Cancun's beaches beckon you at vacation time? Whatever your reasons for wanting to learn the language, this book will help you achieve quick and easy results.

You will learn pronunciation and grammar painlessly and effortlessly without sacrificing speed and accuracy. Whether you're a student, a traveler, or a business person, this book will teach you the basics while giving you the vocabulary and the phrases you'll find most useful in almost every conceivable daily situation. You'll be introduced to a wide variety of topics: food, clothing, sports, health, and much more.

This book is not merely a phrase book, a grammar text, or a travel guide—it's a combination of all three. That makes it not only very unique but an extremely useful tool for people who want a working command of the Spanish language. It will allow you to understand and to be understood without embarrassment or frustration and with ease and enjoyment. Yes, learning Spanish can be fun!

This book was written with you in mind. That's why it's so user-friendly. By the time you've read it through, you'll be a pro at ordering a meal to suit your diet, watching a Spanish film without depending on the subtitles, finding the perfect meringue partner, replacing the contact lens you lost while scuba diving, and even buying a time-share property in South America with ease and confidence. You'll be amazed and surprised at how rapidly you'll learn what you need to know.

In addition to all the vocabulary lists, phrases, grammatical explanations, references, and pronunciation guides, this book contains lots of extras presented in sidebars throughout the text:

Something Extra

Look here for extra tips and hints about the language and customs of Spanish-speaking people and for reminders on how to say it right.

¡Cuidado!

Watch out! These boxes indicate pitfalls and traps you want to sidestep. Remember, you want to avoid sounding and acting like a gringo.

Fast Forward

These sidebars present useful suggestions and activities that allow you to quickly and efficiently get the most out of the material presented to you. Use these ideas to increase your vocabulary and to perfect your speaking and communication skills.

Dedication

This book is dedicated to my patient, proofreader husband, Douglas; my skilled, computer-consultant son, Eric; my most ardent fan and son, Michael; and my parents, Sara and Jack Bernstein, whose love and support have helped me become the woman I am today.

Acknowledgments

Thank you! Thank you! Thank you to some very special people who have made a difference in my life and have greatly enriched it. A special "I love you!" accompanied by hugs and kisses to:

Ray Elias for getting my program up and running, for ensuring that the local bookstores keep Stein in stock, and for being an even greater guy 38 years later;

Werner K. Elias for making an important delivery;

Roger H. Herz for being a dear friend and a cooperative consultant;

Marty Hyman for giving me the best legal advice imaginable;

Marty Leder for making me laugh and for keeping my spirits up;

Chris Levy for being the best advisor and confidante in the world, for always knowing the right thing to do, and for teaching me lessons I needed to learn.

And thanks to the people at Macmillan.

The Gringo's Quick Pronunciation Guide

Even though Spanish is a foreign language, it's very easy to pronounce because it is very phonetic. It's that simple! Just say each word exactly as you see it and add a Spanish accent. Chances are, you'll sound remarkably like a native speaker—well, close to one anyway.

Something Extra

There are four additional letters in Spanish that we do not have in English: ch, ll, ñ, and rr.

Accentuate the Positive

You will notice that there are three accents in Spanish:

➤ The ´ simply indicates that you put more stress on the vowel.

➤ The ˜ only appears over an n. It produces the sound "ny" as in the first n in union. The ñ in considered a separate letter.

➤ The ¨ can be used when there is a diphthong (two vowels together). It indicates that each vowel must be pronounced separately.

¡Cuidado!

All letters in Spanish are pronounced except the letter h, which is always silent. The letter v is pronounced like the English b. The k and the w are used only in words of foreign origin.

Different Strokes for Different Folks

The following pronunciations are for the Spanish spoken is South and Central America and in certain areas of southern Spain.

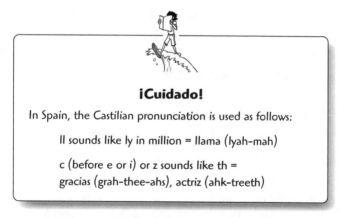

¡Cuidado!

In Spain, the Castilian pronunciation is used as follows:

ll sounds like ly in million = llama (lyah-mah)

c (before e or i) or z sounds like th = gracias (grah-thee-ahs), actriz (ahk-treeth)

Letter	Sound	Example	Pronunciation
Vowels			
a	ah	Ana	ah-nah
e	eh	entrar	ehn-trahr

Letter	Sound	Example	Pronunciation
i	ee	idea	ee-deh-yah
o	oh	oficina	oh-fee-see-nah
u	oo	usar	oo-sahr

Diphthongs (Vowel Combinations)

Letter	Sound	Example	Pronunciation
ae	ah-yeh	aeropuerto	ah-yeh-roh-pwehr-toh
ai	ah-yee	aire	ah-yee-reh
au	ow	auto	ow-toh
ay	ah-yee	hay	ah-yee
ea	eh-yah	reacción	rreh-yahk-see-yohn
ei	eh-yee	beisból	beh-yees-bohl
eo	eh-yoh	feo	feh-yoh
eu	eh-yoo	Europa	eh-yoo-roh-pah
ey	eh-yee	rey	rreh-yee
ia	ee-yah	Gloria	gloh-ree-yah
ie	ee-yeh	fiesta	fee-yehs-tah
io	ee-yoh	avión	ah-bee-yohn
iu	ee-yoo	ciudad	see-yoo-dahd
oa	oh-wah	toalla	toh-wah-yah
oe	oh-weh	oeste	oh-wehs-teh
oi	oy	oiga	oy-gah
oy	oy	soy	soy
ua	wah	guardar	gwahr-dahr
ue	weh	cuesta	kwehs-tah
ui	wee	cuidado	kwee-dah-doh
uo	oo-oh	conintuo	kohn-tee-noo-oh
uy	wee	muy	mwee

Consonants

Letter	Sound	Example	Pronunciation
b	b	bueno	bweh-noh

continues

continued

Letter	Sound	Example	Pronunciation
c	soft c (s) before e, i	centro	sehn-troh
	hard c (k) elsewhere	casa	kah-sah
ch	ch	Chile	chee-leh
d	d	dos	dohs
f	f	favor	fah-bohr
g	soft g before e, i	general	heh-neh-rahl
	hard g elsewhere	gracias	grah-see-yahs
h	silent	hombre	ohm-breh
k	k	kilo	kee-loh
l	l	lista	lees-tah
ll	y	llama	yah-mah
m	m	madre	mah-dreh
n	n	nada	nah-dah
ñ	ny	año	ah-nyoh
p	p	padre	pah-dreh
q	k	Quito	kee-toh
r	r (small roll)	salero	sah-leh-roh
rr	r (large roll)	carro	kah-rroh
s	s	sí	see
t	t	toro	toh-roh
v	b (less explosive English b)	vender	behn-dehr
x	s, ks	extra	ehs-trah
		exacto	ehk-sahk-toh
z	s	zoo	so

Something Extra

The Spanish r is always rolled. Give it something extra when the r comes at the beginning of the word. The rr is always rolled a lot (about three trills).

Fast Forward

Think of learning a language as a mental fitness routine. Start slowly and carefully work up to a pace that suits you. Remember, you don't want to burn yourself out during the first workout. Give it your best shot and then practice, practice, practice. You might want to purchase a small, inexpensive cassette recorder to periodically record and playback anything you might want to read or say. In no time flat, you'll notice the improvement you've made. Go for it!

Chapter 1

A Plan of Action

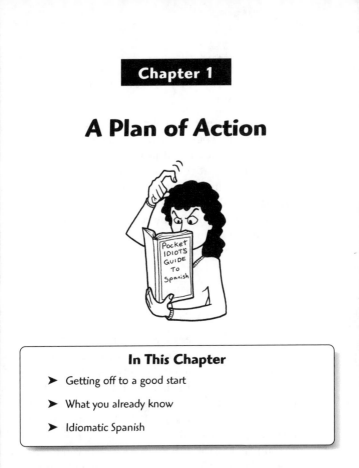

In This Chapter

➤ Getting off to a good start

➤ What you already know

➤ Idiomatic Spanish

So you want to learn Spanish and you want to learn it fast. The easiest and most efficient way to accomplish this goal is just to plunge right in. Totally immerse yourself in anything and everything Spanish. The trick is to have a love affair not only with the language but with the culture as well. Follow these suggestions if you want to quickly develop a long-lasting, fulfilling relationship with Spanish.

➤ Be honest with yourself. What exactly are your goals? How much linguistic ability do you possess? Do you have a good ear for language? Determine how much time each day you want to devote to

Spanish and stick with it. Proceed at your own pace. There's no rush!

➤ One way or another, get your hands on a good bilingual dictionary. Pocket varieties (which usually cost between $6 and $15) might suit the needs of some learners but can prove somewhat deficient for others. Before making a decision, carefully check what is available in your local bookstore or library. The following are among the more popular, easy-to-use, and comprehensive dictionaries, with a wide range of up-to-the-minute, colloquial, and idiomatic words and phrases:

Harper Collins (approximately $55)

Larousse (approximately $60)

➤ Listen to Spanish whenever you can. Never miss an opportunity to become involved with the language. A wide selection of foreign films is available at large video stores. Try not to cheat and read the subtitles. Public service radio and television broadcast many Spanish programs. Look and listen! Borrow language tapes from your local library and pay attention to the sounds of Spanish. Perhaps you can even use a language or computer laboratory at a neighboring school or university.

➤ Read everything you can get your hands on. Read to yourself or out loud to your mirror. Practice your comprehension and your pronunciation all at once. Don't be embarrassed to read children's books, comics, or even fairy tales. They're easy and entertaining! Pick up a Spanish newspaper (*El Diario/La Prensa*, for example) and focus on what's happening in the Hispanic world.

➤ Find the perfect spot in your home to serve as un rincón español (a Spanish corner). Dedicate this area to your new project. Make it look the part. Use posters and articles as decorations. Hang labeled pictures of vocabulary items you want to master. Organize and keep your Spanish materials in this special spot.

Let Us Begin

Your knowledge of Spanish is undoubtedly more extensive than you realize. That's right. You know more than you think. Chocolate, potatoes, tomatoes, taxi, patio, piano, alpaca, mosquito—the list of Spanish words used in English is surprisingly long! You probably don't even realize just how many Spanish words and phrases already are part of your vocabulary. And loads of Spanish words and expressions are so similar to English that you will find them very easy to use and understand with a minimal amount of effort.

Fast Forward

If you ever get stuck for a word you need, just use your body. Think of it as playing charades.

The Cognate Connection

Want to pick up Spanish really quickly? Learn your cognates! What are they? Quite simply, a *cognate* is a word spelled exactly the same (or almost the same) as a word in English and that has the same meaning. Sometimes we've actually borrowed a word from Spanish, letter for letter, and have incorporated it into our own vocabulary. Sure, cognates are pronounced differently in each language, but the meaning of the Spanish word is quite obvious to anyone who speaks English.

Fast Forward

Keep an alphabetical, ongoing list of all the Spanish cognates you know. Practice using them in sentences as often as you can. Pronounce them with your best Spanish accent.

Want to get a jump start on your list? Tables 1.1 and 1.2 provide lists of words that are the same (or almost the same) in both languages.

Table 1.1 Exact Cognates

Adjectives	Masculine Nouns El (ehl)	Feminine Nouns La (lah)
cruel (kroo-ehl)	actor (ahk-tohr)	banana (bah-nah-nah)
grave (grah-beh)	animal (ah-nee-mahl)	fiesta (fee-yehs-tah)
horrible (oh-rree-bleh)	color (koh-lohr)	hotel (oh-tehl)
natural (nah-too-rahl)	hospital (ohs-pee-tahl)	radio (rah-dee-yoh)
tropical (troh-pee-kahl)	motor (moh-tohr)	soda (soh-dah)

Something Extra

All nouns in Spanish have a gender, either masculine or feminine. Use el to express *the* before a masculine singular noun and use la to express *the* before a feminine singular noun. It is generally very easy to determine which to use.

Table 1.2 Almost Exact Cognates

Adjectives	Masculine Nouns El (ehl)	Feminine Nouns La (lah)
ambicioso (ahm-bee-see-yoh-soh)	aniversario (ah-nee-behr-sah-ree-yoh)	aspirina (ahs-pee-ree-nah)
confortable (kohn-fohr-tah-bleh)	automovíl (ow-toh-moh-beel)	bicicleta (bee-see-kleh-tah)
curioso (koo-ree-yoh-soh)	barbero (bahr-beh-roh)	blusa (bloo-sah)
delicioso (deh-lee-see-yoh-soh)	diccionario (deeks-yoh-nah-ree-yoh)	cathedral (kah-teh-drahl)
diferente (dee-feh-rehn-teh)	elefante (eh-leh-fahn-teh)	dieta (dee-yeh-tah)
elegante (eh-leh-gahn-teh)	grupo (groo-poh)	familia (fah-meel-yah)
excelente (ehk-seh-lehn-teh)	menú (meh-noo)	gasolina (gah-soh-lee-nah)
importante (eem-pohr-tahn-teh)	parque (pahr-keh)	guitarra (gee-tah-rrah)
imposible (eem-poh-see-bleh)	plato (plah-toh)	hamburguesa (ahm-boor-geh-sah)
moderno (moh-dehr-noh)	presidente (preh-see-dehn-teh)	lista (lees-tah)

continues

Table 1.2 Continued

Adjectives	Masculine Nouns El (ehl)	Feminine Nouns La (lah)
necesario (neh-seh-sah-ree-yoh)	profesor (proh-feh-sohr)	música (moo-see-kah)
ordinario (ohr-dee-nah-ree-yoh)	programa (proh-grah-mah)	nacionalidad (nah-see-yoh-nah-lee-dahd)
posible (poh-see-bleh)	restaurante (rrehs-tow-rahn-teh)	opinión (oh-pee-nee-yohn)
probable (proh-bah-bleh)	salario (sah-lah-ree-yoh)	persona (pehr-soh-nah)
rico (rree-koh)	teléfono (teh-leh-foh-noh)	turista (too-rees-tah)
sincero (seen-seh-roh)	tigre (tee-greh)	universidad (oo-nee-behr-see-dahd)

Verbs

Verbs (action words) can be cognates too. The majority of Spanish verbs fall into one of three categories: the -ar family, the -er family, and the -ir family. These verbs are considered regular because all verbs in the same family follow the same rules.

You should recognize the following verbs. Don't forget to add them to your growing list of cognates.

AR verbs	ER verbs	IR verbs
acompañar (ah-kohm-pah-nyahr)	comprender (kohm-prehn-dehr)	aplaudir (ah-plow-deer)
celebrar (seh-leh-brahr)	responder (rrehs-pohn-dehr)	decidir (deh-see-deer)
declarar (deh-klah-rahr)	vender (behn-dehr)	describir (dehs-kree-beer)

AR verbs	ER verbs	IR verbs
entrar (ehn-trahr)		persuadir (pehr-swah-deer)
explicar (ehks-plee-kahr)		preferir (preh-feh-reer)
observar (ohb-sehr-bahr)		omitir (oh-mee-teer)
preparar (preh-pah-rahr)		recibir (rreh-see-beer)
usar (oo-sahr)		sufrir (soo-freer)

¡Cuidado!

Beware of words that look like cognates but have a different meaning:

asistir (ah-sees-teer), to attend

caro (kah-roh), expensive

flor (flohr), flower

hay (ahy), there is/are

librería (lee-breh-ree-yah), bookstore

pan (pahn), bread

Idiomatically Speaking

So what exactly is an idiom? In any language, an *idiom* is a particular word or expression whose meaning cannot be readily understood by either its grammar or the words used to express it. Examples of some common English idioms are:

➤ You're driving me crazy!

➤ I have some time to kill.

➤ It's raining cats and dogs.

➤ You'll have to pay through the nose.

You will become acquainted with many Spanish idioms as you go from chapter to chapter.

Fast Forward

Keep handy a list of the idioms you learn in each chapter. Try to use the ones that will be most helpful to you in situations in which you will speak the language.

Chapter 2

Grammar 1–2–3

In This Chapter

➤ Nouns

➤ Verbs

➤ Adjectives

➤ Adverbs

➤ Prepositions

If you really want to speak Spanish like a native, you will be happy to know that speaking a foreign language doesn't mean you'll have to mentally translate pages of rules. Sure, that's how they tried to teach you in school way back when (and it was pure drudgery). With today's communicative approach, however, it's simply not necessary for you to walk around with a dictionary under your arm. On the contrary, it means learning to use the language and its patterns naturally, the way a native speaker does. To do this, you need to know basic grammar as well as the idioms and colloquialisms used by native speakers.

Nouns for Names

Nouns name people, places, things, or ideas. Just like in English, nouns can be replaced by pronouns (such as he, she, it, they). Unlike in English, however, all nouns in Spanish have a gender. This means all nouns have a sex. Did that grab your attention? Sorry to disappoint you, but in this case, sex refers to the masculine or feminine designation of the noun. In Spanish, all nouns also have a number (singular or plural). Little articles (words that stand for "the" or "a") serve as noun identifiers and usually help indicate gender and number. Remember, even if you can't figure out the gender of a noun or if you use the wrong gender or number, you will still be understood as long as you use the correct word.

Gender

Gender is very easy in Spanish. All nouns that refer to males are masculine; those that refer to females are feminine. Use the noun identifiers in Table 2.1 to express "the" or "a":

Table 2.1 Singular Noun Identifiers

	The	A, An, One
Masculine	el	un
Feminine	la	una

Some noun endings make it extremely easy to determine the gender. In general, masculine nouns end in -o and feminine nouns end in -a. Table 3.2 provides a list of endings that can help make the job of gender identification easy.

Something Extra

Some nouns can be either masculine or feminine depending on whether the speaker is referring to a male or female. Just change the article without changing the spelling of the noun:

el artista	la artista
el estudiante	la estudiante
el dentista	la dentista
el joven	la joven

Some nouns are always just masculine or just feminine no matter the sex of the person to whom you are referring:

el bebé	la persona

Table 2.2   Gender Identification Made Easy

Masculine Endings	Example	Feminine Endings	Example
-o	carro	-a	fiesta
-ema	problema	-ión	porción
-consonants (usually)	limón	-dad	oportunidad
		-tad	amistad
		-tud	juventud
		-umbre	costumbre
		-ie	serie

Of course, there are always exceptions to the rule—just make sure you don't get lazy, sloppy, and over-confident. Keep the following exceptions in mind for future use:

➤ Masculine nouns that end in -a:

  el clima (ehl klee-mah), the climate

  el día (ehl dee-yah), the day

  el idioma (ehl ee-dee-yoh-mah), the language

  el mapa (ehl mah-pah), the map

  el problema (ehl proh-bleh-mah), the problem

  el programa (ehl proh-grah-mah), the program

  el telegrama (ehl teh-leh-grah-mah), the telegram

➤ Feminine nouns that end in -o

  la mano (lah mah-noh), the hand

  la radio (lah rrah-dee-yoh), the radio

  la foto, short for fotografía (lah foh-toh), the photo

  la moto, short for motocicleta (lah moh-toh), the motorcycle

Number

When a Spanish noun refers to more than one person, place, thing, or idea, it must be made plural—just like in English. Table 2.3 shows that it is not enough to simply change the noun. The identifying article must be made plural as well.

Table 2.3 Plural Articles

	The	Some
Masculine	los	unos
Feminine	las	unas

Forming the plural of nouns in Spanish is really quite easy. All you have to do is add -s to a singular noun that ends in a vowel, and add -es to a singular noun that ends in a consonant.

el muchacho	los muchachos	el autor	los autores
la muchacha	las muchachas	la ciudad	las ciudades

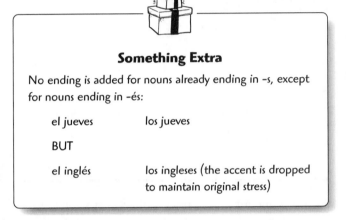

Something Extra

No ending is added for nouns already ending in -s, except for nouns ending in -és:

el jueves	los jueves
BUT	
el inglés	los ingleses (the accent is dropped to maintain original stress)

¡Cuidado!

For nouns ending in -z, change the z to c before adding -es:

el pez	los peces
una actriz	unas actrices

Verbs in Action

Verbs are words that indicate actions or states of being. Verbs require a subject, whether it is expressed in a statement or implied in a command. Subjects can be nouns or pronouns and, just like in English, they are given a person and a number as shown in Table 2.4.

Table 2.4   Subject Pronouns

Person	Singular	Plural
first	yo (yoh), I	nosotros (noh-soh-trohs), we
second	tú (too), you	vosotros (boh-soh-trohs), you
third	él (ehl), he	ellos (eh-yohs), they
	ella (eh-yah), she	ellas (ehl), they
	usted (Ud.)(oo-stehd), you	ustedes (Uds.) (oo-steh-dehs), you

Subject pronouns are not used as often in Spanish as they are in English. This is because the verb ending usually quite clearly identifies the subject.

To speak about a group of women, use nosotras or vosotras or ellas. When speaking about a mixed group, always use the masculine plural—regardless of the number of males in the group.

Tú is used when speaking to a relative, a close friend, a child, or a pet. In all other instances, use the polite form Ud. The vosotros form is used primarily in Spain. In Spanish-speaking South America and the Caribbean, the Uds. form is used.

Verbs are generally shown as an infinitive, the basic "to" form of the verb: to live, to laugh, to love. An infinitive, whether in Spanish or in English, is the form of the verb before it has been conjugated. In English, we conjugate verbs all the time without even paying attention to the fact that we're doing it. Conjugation refers to changing the ending of a verb so it agrees with the subject. Verbs can be regular (most verbs with the same ending follow the same rules) or irregular (there are no rules so you must memorize them).

Regular verbs in Spanish belong to one of three large families—verbs whose infinitives end in -ar, -er, or -ir. The verbs within each family are conjugated in exactly the same manner. After you've learned the pattern for one family, you know them all.

Subject	-ar verbs (hablar)	-er verbs (comer)	-ir verbs (abrir)
yo	hablo	como	abro
tú	hablas	comes	abres
el, ella, Ud.	habla	come	abre
nosotros	hablamos	comemos	abrimos
vosotros	habláis	coméis	abrís
ellos, ellas, Uds.	hablan	comen	abren

Fast Forward

Do you want to increase your vocabulary quickly? If you do, you should have as many verbs as possible on the tip of your tongue. Paste the following verb tables to your refrigerator. Every time you open the door, pick five verbs to learn.

Verb Tables

Tables 2.5, 2.6, and 2.7 provide practical lists of the most frequently used -ar, -er, and -ir verbs. These are the ones you'll use the most in any given situation.

Table 2.5 Common –ar Verbs

Verb	Pronunciation	Meaning
acompañar	ah-kohm-pah-nyahr	to accompany
alquilar	ahl-kee-lahr	to rent
aterrizar	ah-tehr-ree-sar	to land
ayudar	ah-yoo-dahr	to help
buscar	boos-kahr	to look for
cambiar	kahm-bee-yahr	to change
cantar	kahn-tahr	to sing
comprar	kohm-prahr	to buy
desear	deh-seh-yahr	to desire
enseñar	ehn-sehn-nyahr	to teach, to show
entrar	ehn-trahr	to enter
enviar	ehn-bee-yahr	to send
escuchar	ehs-koo-chahr	to listen (to)
esperar	ehs-peh-rahr	to hope, to wait for
estudiar	ehs-too-dee-yahr	to study
explicar	ehks-plee-kahr	to explain
firmar	feer-mahr	to sign
ganar	gah-nahr	to win, to earn
hablar	hahb-lahr	to speak, to talk
invitar	een-bee-tahr	to invite
lavar	lah-bahr	to wash
llegar	yeh-gahr	to arrive
mirar	mee-rahr	to look at

Verb	Pronunciation	Meaning
nadar	nah-dahr	to swim
necesitar	neh-seh-see-tahr	to need
notar	noh-tahr	to note
pagar	pah-goh	to pay
pasar	pah-sahr	to spend (time)
preguntar	preh-goon-tahr	to ask
presentar	preh-sehn-tahr	to introduce
prestar	prehs-tahr	to lend
regresar	rreh-greh-sahr	to return
reparar	rreh-pah-rahr	to repair
reservar	rreh-sehr-bahr	to reserve
telefonear	teh-leh-foh-neh-yahr	to phone
terminar	tehr-mee-nahr	to end
tirar	tee-rahr	to pull
tocar	toh-kahr	to touch, to play (an instrument)
tomar	toh-mahr	to take
usar	oo-sahr	to use, to wear
viajar	bee-yah-hahr	to travel
visitar	bee-see-tahr	to visit

Table 2.6 Common -er Verbs

Verb	Pronunciation	Meaning
aprender	ah-prehn-dehr	to learn
beber	beh-behr	to drink
comer	koh-mehr	to eat
comprender	kohm-prehn-dehr	to understand

continues

Table 2.6   **Continued**

Verb	Pronunciation	Meaning
creer	kreh-yehr	to believe
deber	deh-behr	to have to, to owe
leer	leh-yehr	to read
responder	rrehs-pohn-dehr	to respond
vender	behn-dehr	to sell

Table 2.7   **Common –ir Verbs**

Verb	Pronunciation	Meaning
abrir	ah-breer	to open
asistir	ah-sees-teer	to attend
decidir	deh-see-deer	to decide
describir	dehs-kree-beer	to describe
escribir	ehs-kree-beer	to write
recibir	rreh-see-beer	to receive
subir	soo-beer	to go up, to climb
vivir	bee-beer	to live

Adjectives at Work

Adjectives help to describe nouns. Unlike in English, in Spanish all adjectives agree in number and gender with the nouns they modify. In other words, in a Spanish sentence, all the words have to match. If the noun is singular, its adjective must also be singular. If the noun is feminine, you must be sure to give the correct feminine form of the adjective.

With most adjectives, you can form the feminine by simply Changing the -o of the masculine form to an -a, as shown in Table 2.8.

Fast Forward

Use the adjectives in Table 2.8 to describe your family members and friends. Every day, choose one person and use as many adjectives as you can to describe him or her.

Table 2.8 Forming Feminine Adjectives

Masculine	Pronunciation	Feminine	Meaning
alto	ahl-toh	alta	tall
bajo	bah-hoh	baja	short
bonito	boh-nee-toh	bonita	pretty
bueno	bweh-noh	buena	good
delgado	dehl-gah-doh	delgada	thin
delicioso	deh-lee-see-yoh-soh	deliciosa	delicious
divertido	dee-behr-tee-doh	divertida	fun
feo	feh-yoh	fea	ugly
flaco	flah-koh	flaca	thin
gordo	gohr-doh	gorda	fat
guapo	gwah-poh	guapa	pretty
magnífico	mahg-nee-fee-koh	magnífica	magnificent
malo	mah-loh	mala	bad
moreno	moh-reh-noh	morena	dark-haired
nuevo	nweh-boh	nueva	new
ordinario	ohr-dee-nah-ree-yoh	ordinaria	ordinary
pelirrojo	peh-lee-rroh-hoh	pelirroja	redheaded
pequeño	peh-keh-nyoh	pequeña	small

continues

Table 2.8 Continued

Masculine	Pronunciation	Feminine	Meaning
rico	rree-koh	rica	rich
rubio	rroo-bee-yoh	rubia	blond
serio	seh-ree-yoh	seria	serious
simpático	seem-pah-tee-koh	simpática	nice
sincero	seen-seh-roh	sincera	sincere
tímido	tee-mee-doh	tímida	shy
viejo	bee-yeh-hoh	vieja	old

The adjectives in Table 2.9 end in -e, -a, or a consonant. It is not necessary to make any changes to get the feminine form.

Table 2.9 Adjectives

Adjective	Pronunciation	Meaning
Adjectives ending in -e		
alegre	ah-leh-greh	happy
amable	ah-mah-bleh	nice
elegante	eh-leh-gahn-teh	elegant
excelente	ehks-seh-lehn-teh	excellent
grande	grahn-deh	big
importante	eem-pohr-tahn-teh	important
independiente	een-deh-pehn-dee-yehn-teh	independent
inteligente	een-teh-leh-gehn-teh	intelligent
interesante	een-teh-reh-sahn-teh	interesting
pobre	poh-breh	poor
responsable	rrehs-pohn-sah-bleh	responsible
triste	trees-teh	sad

Adjective	Pronunciation	Meaning
Adjectives ending in -a		
egoísta	eh-goh-ees-tah	selfish
idealista	ee-deh-yah-lees-tah	idealistic
materialista	mah-teh-ree-yah-lees-tah	materialistic
optimista	ohp-tee-mees-tah	optimistic
pesimista	peh-see-mees-tah	pessimistic
realista	rree-yah-lees-tah	realistic
Adjectives ending in a consonant		
cortés	kohr-tehs	courteous
cruel	kroo-ehl	cruel
difícil	dee-fee-seel	difficult
fácil	fah-seel	easy
joven	hoh-behn	young
popular	poh-poo-lahr	popular

In English, adjectives generally are placed before the nouns they modify (for example, the tall man). In Spanish, however, most adjectives come after the nouns the describe (for example, el hombre grande). Don't let this bother you. If you make a mistake, you'll still be understood.

Adverbs in Use

Adverbs are words that describe verbs, adjectives, or other adverbs. In English, most adverbs end in -ly (for example, he dances slowly). In Spanish, they end in -mente (for example, èl baila rápidamente). Adverbs probably will pose few problems as you learn the language.

¡Cuidado!

Masculine adjectives ending in -or add an -a to form the feminine:

encantador   encantadora

Adjectives showing nationality that end in a consonant add -a and may drop an accent to form the feminine:

inglés   inglesa

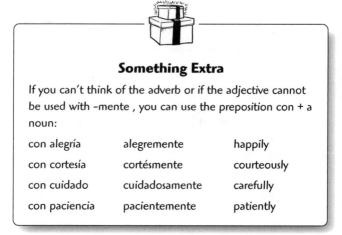

Something Extra

If you can't think of the adverb or if the adjective cannot be used with -mente , you can use the preposition con + a noun:

con alegría	alegremente	happily
con cortesía	cortésmente	courteously
con cuidado	cuidadosamente	carefully
con paciencia	pacientemente	patiently

To form adverbs, simply add -mente to the feminine, singular form of the adjective. Remember to look for the letter at the end of the adjective and pay attention to selecting the correct feminine form. Table 2.10 will show you how to do this.

Table 2.10 Adverbs Formed from Feminine Adjectives

Masculine—adj.	Feminine—adj.	Adverb	Meaning
completo	completa	completamente	completely
especial	especial	especialmente	especially
final	final	finalmente	finally
frecuente	frecuente	frecuentemente	frequently
lento	lenta	lentamente	slowly
rápido	rápida	rápidamente	quickly

Fast Forward

Make a list of five things you like to do and how well you do them. Practice reading your list aloud.

Something Extra

When you find it necessary to describe an action with two or more adverbs, add -mente only to the last one. The other adverbs should be shown in the feminine, singular adjective form. It is assumed that -mente would have been added had they stood alone.

Enrique habla clara, lenta, fácil, y elocuentemente.

Henry speaks clearly, slowly, easily, and eloquently.

Prepositions

Prepositions show the relationship between a noun and another word in a sentence. Table 2.11 shows common prepositions you will find very useful.

Table 2.11 Prepositions

Preposition	Pronunciation	Meaning
a	ah	to, at
además de	ah-deh mahs deh	in addition to, besides
al lado de	ahl lah-doh deh	at the side of, beside
alrededor (de)	ahl-reh-deh-dohr (deh)	around
antes (de)	ahn-tehs (deh)	before
cerca (de)	sehr-kah (deh)	near
con	kohn	with
contra	kohn-trah	against
de	deh	of, from, about
debajo (de)	deh-bah-hoh (deh)	under
delante (de)	deh-lahn-teh (deh)	in front (of)
dentro (de)	dehn-troh (deh)	within, inside of
después (de)	dehs-pwehs (deh)	after
detrás (de)	deh-trahs (deh)	behind, in back (of)
en	ehn	in
encima (de)	ehn-see-mah (deh)	above
enfrente de	ehn frehn-teh deh	in front of, opposite, facing
entre	ehn-treh	between, among
en vez de	ehn behs deh	instead of
frente a	frehn-teh ah	opposite, facing

Preposition	Pronunciation	Meaning
fuera de	fweh-rah deh	outside of
hacia	ah-see-yah	toward
hasta	ahs-tah	up to, until
lejos (de)	leh-hohs (deh)	far (from)
para	pah-rah	for, in order to
por	pohr	by, through
según	seh-goon	according to
sin	seen	without
sobre	soh-breh (delete this)	on, upon

¡Cuidado!

In certain cases, contractions form with the prepositions a and de, whether they are used alone or as part of a longer expression.

a + el = al

de + el + del

Hablo *al* hombre.
I speak *to* the man.

Hablo *del* hombre.
I speak *about* the man.

There are no contractions with la, los, and las.

Hablo a la muchacha, a los hombres, y a las mujeres.
I speak to the girl, the men, and the women.

The following pronouns are used after prepositions:

mí	me	**nosotros(as)**	us
ti	you	**vosotros(as)**	you
él	him	**ellos**	them
ella	her	**ellas**	them
Ud.	you	**Uds.**	you

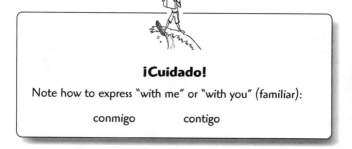

¡Cuidado!

Note how to express "with me" or "with you" (familiar):

conmigo	contigo

Chapter 3

All About You

In This Chapter

➤ Greetings and salutations

➤ Ser versus estar

➤ Professions

➤ Countries

➤ Family members

➤ Possession

➤ Tener

➤ Asking questions

The best way to learn a foreign language is to find a friend who is a sympathetic native speaker and then just jabber away. Talk about anything and everything that strikes your fancy. Ask to be helped and corrected. Don't be shy about using a dictionary or about asking for help with unfamiliar words. To develop a friendship, you have to talk about yourself and ask about your newfound friend. Don't be shy. Strike up a conversation using some or all of the following phrases as your opening lines:

Spanish	Pronunciation	Meaning
Buenos días	bweh-nohs dee-yahs	Hello
Buenas tardes	bweh-nahs tahr-dehs	Good afternoon
Buenas noches	bweh-nahs noh-chehs	Good evening
Señor	seh-nyohr	Sir
Señorita	seh-nyoh-ree-tah	Miss
Señora	seh-nyoh-rah	Mrs.
Me llamo . . .	meh yah-moh	My name is . . . (I call myself)
¿Cómo se llama?	koh-moh seh yah-mah	What is your name?
¿Cómo está Ud.?	koh-moh ehs-tah oo-stehd	How are you?
Muy bien	mwee byehn	Very well
Regular	rreh-goo-lahr	So-so
Así, así	ah-see ah-see	So-so
Más o menos	mahs oh meh-nohs	So-so

Most people love to talk about themselves. Engaging in a friendly conversation in which the other person can be the center of attention is always very pleasant. To ask and answer even the simplest questions in Spanish, you need to know the verbs that express "to be"—ser and estar. These verbs are irregular, and all of their forms must be memorized if you want to use them correctly.

SER	ESTAR
yo soy (soy)	yo estoy (ehs-toy)
tú eres (eh-rehs)	tú estás (ehs-tahs)
él, ella, Ud. es (ehs)	él, ella, Ud. está (ehs-tah)
nosotros somos (soh-mohs)	nosotros estamos (ehs-tah-mohs)
vosotros sois (soys)	vosotros estáis (ehs-tahys)
ellos, ellas, Uds. son (sohn)	ellos, ellas, Uds. están (ehs-tahn)

1. Expresses origin, nationality, or an inherent characteristic or condition of the subject:

Yo soy de España.
I'm from Spain.

Yo soy americana.
I'm American.

Yo soy alto.
I'm tall.

2. Identifies a subject or its traits that will probably remain the same for a long period of time:

Mi padre es doctor.
My father is a doctor.

3. Expresses times and dates:

Son las tres.
It's 3 o'clock.

Es el tres de mayo.
It's May 3.

4. Expresses possession:

Es mi coche.
It's my car.

Es de Marta.
It's Martha's.

5. Is used in impersonal expressions:

Es necesario estudiar.
It's necessary to study.

1. Expresses a temporary state or quality that will not change:

Yo estoy cansado.
I'm tired.

2. Expresses location:

El hotel está allá.
The hotel is there.

3. Forms the progressive tenses:

Estoy escuchando.
I'm listening.

And What's Your Line?

Now that you've mastered the verbs ser and estar, you can easily chat about yourself. Use Table 3.1 to refer to your profession.

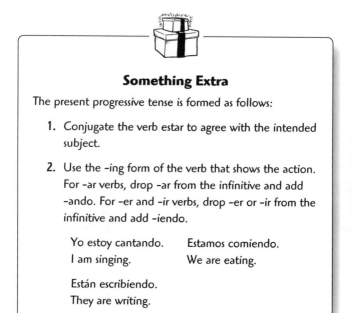

Something Extra

The present progressive tense is formed as follows:

1. Conjugate the verb estar to agree with the intended subject.

2. Use the -ing form of the verb that shows the action. For -ar verbs, drop -ar from the infinitive and add -ando. For -er and -ir verbs, drop -er or -ir from the infinitive and add -iendo.

Yo estoy cantando.   Estamos comiendo.
I am singing.   We are eating.

Están escribiendo.
They are writing.

Table 3.1   Professions

Profession	Spanish	Pronunciation
accountant	contable (m. or f.)	kohn-tah-bleh
business man	hombre de negocios	ohm-breh deh neh-goh-see-yohs
dentist	dentista (m.)	dehn-tees-tah
doctor	doctor (m.)	dohk-tor
engineer	ingeniero	een-heh-nee-yeh-roh

Profession	Spanish	Pronunciation
firefighter	bombero	bohm-beh-roh
government employee	empleado del gobierno	ehm-pleh-yah-doh dehl goh-bee-yehr-noh
hairdresser	barbero	bahr-beh-roh
jeweler	joyero	hoh-yeh-roh
lawyer	abogado	ah-boh-gah-doh
nurse	enfermero	ehn-fehr-meh-roh
police officer	agente de policía (m.)	ah-hen-teh deh poh-lee-see-yah
postal worker	cartero	kahr-teh-roh
programmer	programador	proh-grah-mah-dohr
salesperson	vendedor	behn-deh-dohr
secretary	secretario	seh-kreh-tah-ree-yoh
student	estudiante (m. or f.)	ehs-too-dee-yahn-teh
teacher	profesor	proh-feh-sohr
waiter	camarero	kah-mah-reh-roh
waitress	camarera	kah-mah-reh-rah

¡Cuidado!

To make a profession feminine:

If the profession ends in -o, change the ending to -a.

If the profession ends in -or, add -a.

If the profession ends in -a or -e, no change is necessary.

Where Are You from?

Travelers usually are very curious to know where other travelers come from, especially if they detect a foreign accent. Faraway lands always seem so exotic and exciting, and people love to talk about their hometowns. Use the verb ser + de + the name of your country to say where you are from. Table 3.2 will help you express yourself quite easily.

Table 3.2   Countries Around the World

Country	Spanish	Pronunciation
Belgium	Bélgica	behl-hee-kah
Canada	el Canadá	ehl kah-nah-dah
Denmark	Dinamarca	dee-nah-mahr-kah
Egypt	Egipto	eh-heep-toh
England	Inglaterra	een-glah-teh-rah
Finland	Finlandia	feen-lahn-dee-yah
France	Francia	frahn-see-yah
Germany	Alemania	ah-leh-mah-nee-yah
Greece	Grecia	greh-see-yah
Hungary	Hungría	oon-gree-yah
Ireland	Irlanda	eer-lahn-dah
Italy	Italia	ee-tahl-yah
Japan	el Japón	ehl hah-pohn
Morocco	el Marruecos	ehl mah-rroo-eh-kohs
Netherlands	los Países Bajos	lohs pah-yee-sehs bah-hohs
Norway	Noruega	nohr-oo-eh-gah
Poland	Polonia	poh-loh-nee-yah
Romania	Rumanía	rroo-mah-nee-yah
Russia	Rusia	rroo-see-yah

Country	Spanish	Pronunciation
Scotland	Escocia	ehs-koh-see-yah
Spain	España	ehs-pah-nyah
Sweden	Suecia	soo-eh-see-yah
Switzerland	Suiza	soo-wee-sah
Tunisia	Túnez	too-nehs
Turkey	Turquía	toor-kee-yah
United States	los Estados Unidos	lohs ehs-tah-dohs oo-nee-dohs

And Now for the Loved Ones

No introductory conversation is complete without opening your wallet and showing photos of those you hold near and dear to your heart. Surprisingly, many people enjoy these corny pictures of your family members. Use Table 3.3 to identify everyone correctly.

Table 3.3   Family Members

Family Member	Pronunciation	Meaning
abuelo	ah-bweh-loh	grandfather
abuela	ah-bweh-lah	grandmother
padrino	pah-dree-noh	godfather
padrina	pah-dree-nah	godmother
padre	pah-dreh	father
madre	mah-dreh	mother
padastro	pah-dahs-troh	stepfather
padastra	pah-dahs-trah	stepmother
hijo	ee-hoh	son, child
hija	ee-hah	daughter

continues

Table 3.3 Continued

Family Member	Pronunciation	Meaning
hermano	ehr-mah-noh	brother
hermana	ehr-mah-nah	sister
hermanastro	ehr-mah-nehs-troh	stepbrother
hermanastra	ehr-mah-nehs-trah	stepsister
primo	pree-moh	cousin
prima	pree-mah	cousin (female)
sobrino	soh-bree-noh	nephew
sobrina	soh-bree-nah	niece
tío	tee-yoh	uncle
tía	tee-yah	aunt
nieto	nee-yeh-toh	grandson
nieta	nee-yeh-tah	granddaughter
suegro	sweh-groh	father-in-law
suegra	sweh-grah	mother-in-law
yerno	yehr-noh	son-in-law
nuera	nweh-rah	daughter-in-law
cuñado	koo-nyah-doh	brother-in-law
cuñada	koo-nyah-dah	sister-in-law
novio	noh-bee-yoh	boyfriend
novia	noh-bee-yah	girlfriend

Something Extra

Here are some useful plurals and their spellings:

Table 3.4   Plurals of Family Names

Family Member	Pronunciation	Meaning
hijos	ee-hohs	children
padres	pah-drehs	parents
abuelos	ah-bweh-lohs	grandparents
suegros	sweh-grohs	in-laws
parientes	pah-ree-yehn-tehs	relatives
padrinos	pah-dree-nohs	godparents

You Belong to Me

To show possession in English, we use 's or s' after a noun. There are no apostrophes in Spanish, however. To translate "Julio's mother" into Spanish, a speaker would have to say "the mother of Julio," which is "la madre de Julio." The preposition *de* means of and is used to express possession or relationship.

Possessive adjectives also can be used to show possession, as shown in Table 3.5.

Table 3.5 Possessive Adjectives

| Used Before Masculine Nouns | | Used Before Feminine Nouns | | |
Singular	Plural	Singular	Plural	English
mi	mis	mi	mis	my
tu	tus	tu	tus	your
su	sus	su	sus	his, her, your, its
nuestro	nuestros	nuestra	nuestras	our
vuestro	vuestros	vuestra	vuestras	your
su	sus	su	sus	their

¡Cuidado!

A possessive adjective should agree with the item possessed not the possessor.

| Es mi tía. | Son mis hijos. |
| That's my aunt. | They are my sons. |

This Is What I Have

Perhaps you would like to discuss how many children you have or your age. You also might want to tell how you feel at a particular moment. The verb you will find most helpful in these situations is tener (to have). Like the verbs ser and estar, tener is an irregular verb. All its forms (as seen in Table 3.6) must be memorized.

Table 3.6   Conjugating Tener (to Have)

Conjugated Form of Tener	Pronunciation	Meaning
Yo tengo	tehn-goh	I have
Tú tienes	tee-yeh-nehs	You have
Él, ella, Ud. tiene	tee-yeh-neh	He, she, one has
Nosotros tenemos	teh-neh-mohs	We have
Vosotros tenéis	teh-neh-yees	You have
Ellos, ellas, Uds. tienen	tee-yeh-nehn	They have

Idioms with Tener

The idiomatic expressions in Table 3.7 are used quite frequently in everyday conversation.

Table 3.7   Idioms with Tener

Idiom	Pronunciation	Expression
tener calor	teh-nehr kah-lohr	to be hot
tener dolor de	teh-nehr doh-lohr deh	to have an ache in
tener frío	teh-nehr free-yoh	to be cold
tener ganas de + infinitive	teh-nehr gah-nahs deh	to feel like
tener hambre	teh-nehr ahm-breh	to be hungry
tener miedo de	teh-nehr mee-yeh-doh deh	to be afraid of
tener que + infinitive	teh-nehr keh	to have to
tener razón	teh-nehr rrah-sohn	to be right
tener sed	teh-nehr sehd	to be thirsty
tener sueño	teh-nehr sweh-nyoh	to be sleepy
tener . . . años	teh-nehr ah-nyohs	to be . . . years old

¡Cuidado!

Make sure to conjugate the verb when you use it in context.

> Yo tengo veinte años.
> I'm 20 years old.

Fast Forward

I want to know all about you and my English is poor. Tell me as much as you can about yourself and your family in Spanish. I'm very nosy, so don't leave out any details. Practice what you want to say until it flows smoothly.

Asking Questions

If your Spanish is not quite as perfect as you'd like, you'll probably be content to ask people simple yes or no questions. Besides, that way you won't look too nosy.

Intonation

The easiest way to show that you are asking a question is simply to change your intonation by raising your voice at the end of the sentence.

> ¿Eres americano?

¡Cuidado!

Spanish uses two question marks for every question. Put an upside down question mark at the beginning of the question and a standard one at the end.

Tags

Another simple way to ask a question is to add a tag such as ¿verdad?, ¿no?, or ¿está bien? to the end of a statement. These tags can mean really?, isn't that so?, is it?, isn't it?, are you?, aren't you, do you?, don't you?, all right? or OK?

Eres americano, ¿verdad? (¿no?, ¿está bien?)

You're American, right? (isn't that so?, aren't you?)

Inversion

Inversion means reversing the word order of the subject pronoun and the conjugated verb form.

¿Eres tú americano?

Getting the Scoop

If you're anything like me, a simple yes or no answer never suffices. You want to get the whole picture, and for that, you'll need the facts. Use the questions in Table 3.8 to get all the information you want.

Table 3.8 Information Questions

Word/Phrase	Pronunciation	Meaning
adónde	ah-dohn-deh	to where
a qué hora	ah keh oh-rah	at what time
a quién	ah kee-yehn	to whom
a qué	ah keh	to what
con quién	kohn kee-yehn	with whom
con qué	kohn keh	with what
cuál	kwahl	which
de quién	deh kee-yehn	of, about, from whom
de qué	deh keh	of, about, from what
cuánto	kwahn-toh	how much, many
cómo	koh-moh	how
dónde	dohn-deh	where
de dónde	deh dohn-deh	from where
por qué	pohrkeh	why
cuándo	kwahn-doh	when
quién	kee-yehn	who, whom
qué	keh	what

The easiest way to ask for information is to put the question word immediately before the verbal phrase or thought.

> ¿**Con quién** viaja Ud.?   With whom are you traveling?

¿Qué? asks what? when referring to a description, a definition, or an explanation and asks which? when used before a noun.

¿**Qué** es esto?   ¿**Qué** estás comiendo?
What's that?   What are you eating?

¿**Qué** programa miras?
Which program are you watching?

¿Cuál? and ¿Cuáles? generaly ask which? They ask what?
before the verb ser (to be), except when asking for the
definition of a word (when ¿qué? is used). They ask which
(one)? before the preposition de.

¿**Cuál** es su nombre?   ¿**Cuáles** quieres?
What's your name?   Which (ones) do you want?

¿**Cuál** de los dos prefieres?
Which (one) of the two do you prefer?

In Spanish, all words that ask questions have accent
marks. This distinguishes them from words that are
spelled the same but that state information rather than
asking for it.

¿**Dónde** vives?   Yo no sé **donde** tú vives.
Where do you live?   I don't know where you live.

Something Extra

When followed by a noun, cuánto is used as an adjective
and must agree in number and gender with the noun:

¿Cuánto dinero tienes?   ¿Cuántas muchachas cantan?
How much money   How many girls are singing?
do you have?

Fast Forward

Now it's your turn to be nosy. Write down a list of questions you would like to ask me. I'm a very interesting person, and I have a large family.

Chapter 4

Navigating the Airport

In This Chapter

➤ On the airplane and in the airport

➤ All about ir (to go)

➤ Giving and receiving directions

➤ What to say when you don't understand

So you're planning a trip by plane. Be sure to shop around and compare prices for your ticket. A non-refundable ticket isn't a bargain if you have to change your plans midstream.

Many people are all too well aware that a plane ride can be long and tedious. At times, you might experience minor inconveniences or delays for a wide variety of reasons. During your trip, you might want to change your seat or perhaps ask the flight crew some typical tourist questions. No doubt, if you are traveling on a foreign airline, you might find it helpful to use your knowledge of the language to help you get all the information you need. The terms in Table 4.1 will help you face any problem you might have.

Table 4.1   On the Inside

In-Plane Term	Spanish	Pronunciation
aisle	el pasillo	ehl pah-see-yoh
to board	abordar	ah-bohr-dahr
by the window	cerca de la ventana	sehr-kah deh lah behn-tah-nah
crew	el equipo	ehl eh-kee-poh
to deplane, to exit	salir	sah-leer
emergency exit	la salida de emergencia	lah sah-lee-dah deh eh-mehr-hehn-see-yah
gate	la salida	lah sah-lee-dah
landing	el aterrizaje	ehl ah-teh-rree-sah-heh
life vest	el chaleco salvavidas	ehl chah-leh-koh sahl-bah-bee-dahs
(non) smokers	(no) fumadores	noh foo-mah-doh-rehs
on the aisle	en el pasillo	ehn ehl pah-see-yoh
row	la fila	lah fee-lah
seat	el asiento	ehl ah-see-yehn-toh
seat belt	el cinturón de seguridad	ehl seen-too-rohn deh seh-goo-ree-dahd
to smoke	fumar	foo-mahr
take off	el despegue	ehl dehs-peh-geh
trip	el viaje	ehl bee-yah-heh

The Eagle Has Landed

After you've landed, there should be plenty of signs to point you in the right direction. Where should you go

first? You know it will take your bags a while to be un-
loaded. Do you need to use the bathroom? How about
some foreign currency? After a delicious airline repast, do
you still crave something to eat? Table 4.2 provides all the
words you need to know once you are inside the airport.

Table 4.2 At the Airport

The Place	Spanish	Pronunciation
airline	la aerolínea	lah ah-eh-roh-lee-neh-yah
airplane	el avión	ehl ah-bee-yohn
airport	el aeropuerto	ehl ah-eh-roh-pwehr-toh
arrival	la llegada	lah yeh-gah-dah
baggage claim area	el reclamo de equipage	ehl rreh-klah-moh deh eh-kee-pah-heh
bathrooms	los baños	lohs bah-nyohs
bus stop	la parada de autobús	lah pah-rah-dah deh ow-toh-boos
car rental	el alquiler de carros	ehl ahl-kee-lehr deh kah-rrohs
cart	el carrito	ehl kah-rree-toh
counter	el mostrador	ehl mohs-trah-dohr
customs	la aduana	lah ah-dwah-nah
departure	la salida	lah sah-lee-dah
elevators	los ascensores	lohs ah-sehn-soh-rehs
entrance	la entrada	lah ehn-trah-dah
exit	la salida	lah sah-lee-dah
flight	el vuelo	ehl bweh-loh
gate	la puerta	lah pwehr-tah
information	las informaciónes	lahs een-fohr-mah-see-yoh-nehs
lost and found	la oficina de objetos perdidos	lah oh-fee-see-nah deh ohb-heh-tohs pehr-dee-dohs

continues

Table 4.2 Continued

The Place	Spanish	Pronunciation
to miss the flight	perder el vuelo	pehr-dehr ehl bweh-loh
money exchange	el cambio de dinero	ehl kahm-bee-yoh deh dee-neh-roh
porter	el portero	ehl pohr-teh-roh
stop-over	la escala	lah ehs-kah-lah
suitcase	la maleta	lah mah-leh-tah
ticket	el boleto	ehl boh-leh-toh

Where Are You Going?

It's easy to get lost in sprawling international airports. To get yourself back on track, you need to know how to ask the correct questions. The following question will help you the most:

Use ir + a to express going to a city, state, or country, as follows:

Voy a Nueva York.   I'm going to New York.

Use ir + en to express the many different ways to go someplace, as follows:

Voy a Nueva York   I'm going to New York
  en avión.   by plane.

Note the exception: a pie, on foot.

Voy al cine a pie.

I'm walking (going on foot) to the movies.

¿Dónde está + singular noun?
¿Dónde están + plural noun?

¿Dónde está la salida?   ¿Dónde están los baños?
Where's the exit?   ¿Where are the bathrooms?

One verb that will really come in handy is shown in Table 4.3. Ir (to go) is an irregular verb that must be memorized.

Table 4.3   Conjugating Ir (to Go)

Conjugated Form of Ir	Pronunciation	Meaning
yo voy	boy	I go
tú vas	bahs	you go
él, ella, Ud. va	bah	he, she, one goes
nosotros vamos	bah-mohs	we go
vosotros vais	bahys	you go
ellos, ellas, Uds. van	bahn	they go

Complications

If the place you want to go is not within pointing distance, you'll need other directions. The verbs in Table 4.4 can help you get where you want to go or can help you aide someone else who is lost.

Table 4.4   Giving Directions

Verb	Pronunciation	Meaning
baje(n)	bah-heh(n)	go down
camine(n)	kah-mee-neh(n)	walk
continue(n)	kohn-tee-noo-weh(n)	continue
cruce(n)	kroo-seh(n)	cross
doble(n)	doh-bleh(n)	turn
pase(n)	pah-seh(n)	pass

continues

Table 4.4 Continued

Verb	Pronunciation	Meaning
sea(n)	seh-yah(n)	be
siga(n)	seh-gah(n)	follow, continue
suba(n)	soo-bah(n)	go up
tenga(n)	tehn-gah(n)	have
tome(n)	toh-meh(n)	take
vaya(n)	bah-yah(n)	go

¡Cuidado!

Use either Ud. (singular) or Uds. (plural) as the subject of your command. These are the easiest forms to master. You can use the subject pronoun after the verb. To make the command negative, simply put no before the verb.

Tome (Ud.) el coche.   No crucen (Uds.) la calle.
Take the car.   Don't cross the street.

Por Versus Para

The Spanish words por and para can both mean *for*. Consequently, there is often much confusion about when to use each. You should keep in mind the following rules:

Por Indicates	Para Indicates
motion	destination to a place
Paso *por* la salida.	El avión sale *para* Cuba.
I pass by the exit.	The airplane leaves for Cuba.

Por Indicates	Para Indicates
means, manner Viajo *por* taxi. I travel by taxi.	destination to a recipient Este regalo es *para* mi amigo. This gift is for my friend.
a period of time Duermo *por* la noche. I sleep at night	a time limit La cita es *para* el martes. The appointment is for Tuesday.
frequency, in exchange for Salgo una vez *por* mes. I go out once a month. Son dos plumas *por* $20. They are two pens for $20.	purpose Es un billete *para* el tren. It's a ticket for the train.

What Did You Say?

What if someone gives you directions and you don't understand? Perhaps the person with whom you are speaking is mumbling, is speaking too fast, has a strong accent,
or uses words you don't know. Don't be embarrassed.
The phrases in Table 4.5 can be an invaluable aid if you
need to have something repeated or if you need more
information.

Table 4.5 When You Don't Understand

Expression	Pronunciation	Meaning
Con permiso	kohn pehr-mee-soh	Excuse me
Perdóneme	pehr-doh-neh-meh	Excuse me
Yo no comprendo	yoh noh kom-prehn-doh	I don't understand
Yo no entiendo	yoh noh ehn-tee-yehn-doh	I don't understand
Yo no te oígo	yoh noh teh oy-goh	I don't hear you
Repita por favor	rreh-pee-tah pohr fah-bohr	Please repeat it

continues

Table 4.5 Continued

Expression	Pronunciation	Meaning
Otra vez	oh-trah behs	One more time/again
Hable más despacio	hah-bleh mahs dehs-pah-see-yoh	Speak more slowly
¿Qué dijo?	keh dee-hoh	What did you say?

Fast Forward

Study your phrases and then close this book (but keep your finger on the page). Pretend someone is speaking to you very quickly and you just don't understand. Use as many phrases as you can remember to express your lack of comprehension. You can peek, if you must.

Chapter 5

Getting to Your Destination

In This Chapter

➤ Means of transportation

➤ Cardinal numbers

➤ Telling time

➤ Time expressions

If you're traveling in a Spanish-speaking country, several different means of transportation can get you to your destination. Consider the following: Are you traveling light? If so, you might want to mingle with people and take buses, subways, and trains. How tight is your budget and how much time do you have? If money is no object or if you're in a hurry, a taxi might be your best option. Do you enjoy seeing the countryside? If you're confident and are familiar with traffic laws and street signs, you might just want to rent a car.

Here's how to say how you're getting there:

Yo tomo . . . (yoh toh-moh)   I'm taking . . .

English	Spanish	Pronunciation
the boat	el barco	ehl bahr-koh
the bus	el autobús	ehl ow-toh-boos
the car	el coche	ehl koh-cheh
the car	el automóvil	ehl ow-toh-moh-beel
the car	el carro	ehl kah-rroh
the subway	el metro	ehl meh-troh
the taxi	el taxi	ehl tahk-see
the train	el tren	ehl trehn

If You're Traveling by Bus

The bus system in Madrid is efficient and inexpensive. A bus stop (una parada de autobús, oo-nah pah-rah-dah deh ow-toh-boos) is clearly marked by numbers. Unlike in the U.S., transfers are not free (but bus service is quite inexpensive). Buses don't stop automatically; they must be hailed. A free bus map (un plano de la red, oon plah-noh deh lah rrehd) can easily be obtained at major tourist attractions and hotels.

You might decide not to take a bus if you are touring Mexico City. The buses tend to be very crowded and are more expensive than the subway. You also might find that the routes go all over town and tend to be confusing.

Where is the nearest bus stop?
¿Dónde está la parada de autobús más cercana?
dohn-deh ehs-tah lah pah-rah-dah deh ow-toh-boos
mahs sehr-kah-nah

How much is the fare?
¿Cuánto cuesta el billete?
kwahn-toh kwehs-tah ehl bee-yeh-teh

Do I need exact change?
¿Necesito cambio exacto?
neh-seh-see-toh kahm-bee-yoh ehk-sahk-toh

If You're Traveling by Subway

The subway systems in Madrid and Barcelona can boast of their cleanliness, comfort, safety, and economy. The 11 metro lines in Madrid are easily distinguishable on maps by numbers and different colors. Un plan del metro (oon plahn dehl meh-troh), a subway map, can be conveniently obtained for free at metro stops, hotels, department stores, and tourist offices. The sign "Correspondencia" (koh-rrehs-pohn-dehn-see-yah) indicates that free transfers and connections are available. If you don't exit, you can transfer as often as you like on just one ticket. Navigating the metro is easy—just look at the name of the last stop in the direction you want to go and then follow the signs indicating that station.

Metro tickets are available in single fares (un billete sencillo, oon bee-yeh-teh sehn-see-yoh); as a package of 10 (un billete de diez viajes, oon bee-yeh-teh deh dee-yehs bee-yah-hehs); as tourist tickets (un metrotour de tres días or de cinco días, oon meh-troh-toor deh trehs dee-yahs oh deh seen-koh dee-yahs), which allow unlimited bus, subway, and train transportation for three or five consecutive days (and can be purchased through travel agents, tourist offices, and subway stations); or as a monthly commuter pass (una tarjeta de abono transportes, oo-nah tahr-heh-tah deh ah-bohn-noh trahns-pohr-tehs).

Buenos Aires and Mexico City also have very clean and efficient subway systems in.

Where is the nearest subway?
¿Dónde está la estación de metro más cercana?
dohn-deh ehs-tah lah ehs-tah-see-yohn deh meh-troh
mahs sehr-kah-nah

Where can I buy a ticket?
¿Dónde puedo comprar un billete?
dohn-deh pweh-doh kohm-prahr oon bee-yeh-teh

How much is the fare?
¿Cuánto es la tarifa?
kwahn-toh ehs lah tah-ree-fah

How many more stops are there?
¿Hay cuántas paradas más?
ahy kwahn-tahs pah-rah-dahs mahs

What's the next station?
¿Cuál es la prómixa estación?
kwahl ehs lah prohk-see-mah ehs-tah-see-yohn

Where is there a map?
¿Dónde hay un mapa?
dohn-deh ahy oon mah-pah

If You're Traveling by Taxi

Always try to take a metered taxi so you know exactly
what fare to expect. Surcharges are imposed for luggage
and night and holiday fares. Un gran turismos (grahn too-
rees-mohs) is an unmetered public-service taxi that
charges higher rates. Remember to ask for the fare in advance if this is your choice. In Mexico City, orange-
colored taxis generally are privately owned and can be
called in advance; yellow cabs cruise for passengers. Un
colectivo (oon koh-lehk-tee-boh) is a van or car that can
be shared with other travelers going in the same general
direction.

Where is the nearest taxi stand?
¿Dónde está la parada de taxi más cercana?
dohn-deh ehs-tah lah pah-rah-dah deh tahk-see mahs
sehr-kah-nah

Would you please call me a cab?
¿Puede Ud. conseguirme un taxi, por favor?
pweh-deh oo-stehd kohn-seh-geer-meh oon tahk-see
pohr fah-bohr

I want to go . . .	Stop here.
Quiero ir . . .	Pare aquí.
kee-yeh-roh eer	pah-reh ah-kee
How much is it to . . .	Wait for me.
¿Cuánto cuesta hasta . . .	Espéreme.
kwahn-toh kwehs-tah ahs-tah . . .	ehs-peh-reh-meh

If You're Going by Train

If you're visiting Spain, Red Nacional de Ferrocarriles
Españoles (RENFRE) is the national railroad network of
the country and is comparable to AMTRAK in the United
States. Spain has the most inexpensive train fare in Europe. Nonresidents only can purchase una tarjeta turística
(oo-nah tahr-heh-tah too-rees-tee-kah), which allows unlimited travel in first or second class for 8, 15, or 22 days.
American travelers can purchase a Eurail Pass, which permits unlimited travel rights. The price of this card varies
according to the number of travel days you choose: 15,
25, 40, 60, or 90.

Where is the nearest train station?
¿Dónde está la estacíon de tren más cercana?
dohn-deh ehs-tah lah ehs-tah-see-yohn deh trehn
mahs sehr-kah-nah

I would like . . .
Quisiera . . .
kee-see-yeh-rah

a first (second) class ticket.
un billete de primera (segunda) clase.
oon bee-yeh-teh deh pree-meh-rah
(seh-goon-dah) klah-seh

a round-trip ticket.
un billete de ida y vuelta.
oon bee-yeh-teh deh ee-dah ee bwehl-tah

a (non) smoking compartment.
un departamento para (no) fumadores.
oon deh-pahr-tah-mehn-toh pah-rah (noh)
foo-mah-doh-rehs

Is it a local (express)?
¿Es un tren local (un rápido)?
ehs oon trehn loh-kahl (oon rrah-pee-doh)

From what platform does it leave?
¿De qué andén sale?
deh keh ahn-dehn sah-leh

If You're Traveling by Car

So you're daring enough to go to un alquiler de coches
(oon ahl-kee-lehr deh koh-chehs) to rent a car. Good for
you! Always compare rates before you make a final choice.
Don't be surprised when the price at the gas pump is almost double what you generally pay back home.

I'd like to rent a (give make of car).
Quiero alquilar un _____.
kee-yeh-roh ahl-kee-lahr oon _____

I prefer automatic transmission.
Prefiero el cambio automático.
preh-fee-yeh-roh ehl kahm-bee-yoh ow-toh-mah-
tee-koh

How much does it cost per day (per week)
(per kilometer)?

¿Cuánto cuesta por día (por semana) (por kilómetro)?
kwahn-toh kwehs-tah pohr dee-yah (pohr seh-mah-nah) (por kee-loh-meh-troh)

How much is the insurance?
¿Cuánto es el seguro?
kwahn-toh ehs ehl seh-goo-roh

Is the gas included?
¿Está incluída la gasolina?
ehs-tah een-kloo-eee-doh lah gah-soh-lee-nah

Do you accept credit cards? Which ones?
¿Acepta Ud. tarjetas de crédito? ¿Cuáles?
ahk-sehp-tah oo-steh tahr-heh-tahs deh kreh-dee-toh kwah-lehs

Do you fill it up with gas?
¿Lo llena Ud. con gasolina?
loh lleh-nah kohn gah-soh-lee-nah

¡Cuidado!

If you decide to rent a car, take a tip from me. Carefully inspect the whole car—inside and outside. You never know what might go wrong after you're on the road. Open the trunk and make sure there is a jack—un gato (oon gah-toh)—and a spare tire—una goma de repuesto (oo-nah goh-mah deh rrehs-pwehs-toh).

In Europe, distance is measured in kilometers. Table 5.1 shows the approximate equivalents.

Table 5.1   Distance Measures (Approximate)

Miles	Kilometers
.62	1
3	5
6	10
12	20
31	50
62	100

Heading in the Right Direction

By all means, learn your destination's road signs—some are not as obvious as they should be. Familiarize yourself with the following before you venture out on your own in car:

You also need to know your compass directions.

Meaning	Direction	Pronunciation
to the North	al norte	ahl nohr-teh
to the East	al este	ahl ehs-teh
to the South	al sur	ahl soor
to the West	al oeste	ahl oh-wehs-teh

What's Your Number?

To tell someone which flight or bus you are taking or to figure out how much a rental car is going to set you back, you need to learn the Spanish numbers listed in Table 5.2. Believe it or not, these very same numbers will come in handy when you want to tell time, to count to 10, or to reveal your age.

Fast Forward

Every time you see a number in an ad, practice saying it in Spanish. You'll learn numbers in no time flat.

Table 5.2 Cardinal Numbers

No.	Spanish	Pronunciation	No.	Spanish	Pronunciation
0	cero	seh-roh	4	cuatro	kwah-troh
1	uno	oo-noh	5	cinco	seen-koh
2	dos	dohs	6	seis	seh-yees
3	tres	trehs	7	siete	see-yeh-teh

continues

Table 5.2 Continued

No.	Spanish	Pronunciation	No.	Spanish	Pronunciation
8	ocho	oh-choh	60	sesenta	seh-sehn-tah
9	nueve	noo-weh-beh	70	setenta	seh-tehn-tah
10	diez	dee-yehs	80	ochenta	oh-chen-tah
11	once	ohn-seh	90	noventa	noh-behn-tah
12	doce	doh-seh	100	ciento	see-yehn-toh
13	trece	treh-seh	101 uno	ciento oo-noh	see-yehn-toh
14	catorce	kah-tohr-seh	200	dos cientos	dohs see-yehn-tohs
15	quince	keen-seh	500	quinientos	kee-nee-yehn-tohs
16	diez y seis	dee-yehs ee seh-yees	700	setecientos	seh-teh-see-yehn-tohs
17	diez y siete	dee-yehs ee see-yeh-teh	900	novecientos	noh-beh-see-yehn-tohs
18	diez y ocho	dee-yehs ee oh-choh	1000	mil	meel
19	diez y nueve	dee-yehs ee noo-eh-beh	2000	dos mil	dohs meel
20	veinte	beh-yeen-teh	100,000	cien mil	see-yehn meel
21	veintiuno	beh-yeen-tee-oo-noh	1,000,000	un millión	oon meel-yohn
22	veintidós	beh-yeen-tee-dohs	2,000,000	dos milliones	dohs meel-yoh-nehs
30	treinta	trehn-tah	1,000,000,000	mil millones	meel meel-yoh-nehs
40	cuarenta	kwah-rehn-tah	2,000,000,000	dos mil millones	dohs meel meel-yoh-nehs
50	cincuenta	seen-kwehn-tah			

Something Extra

The Spanish write the number 1 with a little hook on top. To distinguish a 1 from a 7, they put a line through the 7, as in 7.

In numerals and decimals, wherever we use commas, the Spanish use periods (and vice versa).

English	Spanish
1,000	1.000
.25	0,25
$9.95	$9,95

Spanish numbers are not too tricky. Look carefully again at Table 5.2, however, to pick up the following pointers:

➤ The conjunction y (and) is used only for numbers between 16 and 99.

➤ Uno is used only when counting. It becomes un before a masculine noun and una before a feminine noun.

uno, dos, tres . . .	treinta y un muchachos
one, two, three . . .	thirty-one boys
un hombre y una mujer	veinte y una muchachas
a man and a woman	twenty-one girls

➤ The numbers 16–19 and 21–29 are generally written as one word. When this is done, the numbers 16, 22, 23, and 26 have accents:

16	dieciséis	22	veintidós
17	diecisiete	23	veintitrés
21	veintiuno	26	veintiséis

➤ Compounds of ciento (doscientos, trescintos) should agree with a feminine noun.

doscientos hombres	trescientas mujeres
two hundred men	two hundred women

➤ Ciento becomes cien before nouns and before the numbers mil and millones. Before all other numbers, ciento is used.

cien libros	cien mil personas
one hundred books	one hundred thousand people
ciento veinte carros	cien millones de dólares
one hundred and twenty cars	one billion dollars

➤ Although it is not used before ciento or mil, un is used before millón. If a noun follows millón, put *de* between millón and the noun.

ciento pesetas	un millón de habitantes
100 pesetas	1,000,000 inhabitants
mil quinientos años	
1,500 years	

Do You Have the Time?

Now that you have the hang of Spanish numbers, it should be rather easy to express the time, as explained in Table 5.3.

What time is it?	At what time?
¿Qué hora es?	¿A qué hora?
keh oh-rah ehs	ah keh oh-rah

Table 5.3 Time

English	Spanish	Pronunciation
It is 1:00.	Es la una.	ehs lah oo-nah
It is 2:05.	Son las dos y cinco.	sohn lahs dohs ee see-koh
It is 3:10.	Son las tres y diez.	sohn lahs trehs y dee-yehs
It is 4:15.	Son las cuatro y cuarto.	sohn lahs kwah-troh ee kwahr-toh
It is 5:20.	Son las cinco y veinte.	sohn lahs see-koh ee beh-yeen-teh
It is 6:25.	Son las seis y veinti cinco.	sohn lahs seh-yees ee beh-yeen-t-ee seen-koh
It is 7:30.	Son las siete y media.	sohn lahs see-yeh-teh ee meh-dee-yah
It is 7:35 (25 min. to 8).	Son las ocho menos veinte y cinco.	sohn lahs oh-choh meh-nohs behn-teh ee seen-koh
It is 8:40 (20 min.to 9).	Son las nueve menos veinte.	sohn lahs noo-weh-beh meh-nohs beh-yeen-teh
It is 9:45 (15 min. to 10).	Son las diez menos Cuarto.	sohn lahs dee-yehs meh-nohs kwahr-toh
It is 10:50 (10 min. to 11).	Son las once menos diez.	sohn lahs ohn-seh meh-nohs dee-yehs
It is 11:55 (5 min. to noon).	Son las doce menos cinco.	sohn lahns doh-seh meh-nohs seen-koh
It is noon.	El el mediodía.	ehs ehl meh-dee-yoh dee-yah
It is midnight.	Es la medianoche.	ehs lah meh-dee-yah noh-cheh

When telling time make sure you do the following:

➤ Use es for "it is" when saying it is one o'clock. Use son for other numbers because they are plural.

➤ Use the hour + y + the number of minutes to express the time after the hour.

➤ Use the following hour + menos + the number of minutes before that hour whenever it is more than half past the hour.

Son las tres menos cuarto.
It's 2:45.

It also is not unusual to hear the time expressed as follows:

Son las dos y cuarenta y cinco.
It's 2:45.

It's not enough to know how to say what the time is. You might want to know at what time an activity is planned or whether it is taking place in the morning, the afternoon, or the evening. The expressions in Table 5.4 will help you deal with time.

Table 5.4   Time Expressions

Expression	Spanish	Pronunciation
a second	un segundo	oon seh-goon-doh
a minute	un minuto	oon mee-noo-toh
an hour	una hora	oo-nah oh-rah
in the morning (a.m.)	de la mañana	deh lah mah-nyah-nah
in the afternoon (p.m.)	de la tarde	deh lah tahr-deh
in the evening (p.m.)	de la noche	deh lah noh-cheh
at what time	a qué hora	ah keh oh-rah
at exactly 1:00	a la una en punto	ah lah oo-nah ehn poon-toh
at exactly 2:00	a las dos en punto	ah lahs dohs ehn poon-toh

Expression	Spanish	Pronunciation
at about 2:00	a eso de las dos	ah eh-soh deh lahs dohs
a quarter of an hour	un cuarto de hora	oon kwahr-toh deh oh-rah
a half hour	una media hora	oo-nah meh-dee-yah oh-rah
in an hour	en una hora	ehn oo-nah oh-rah
until 2:00	hasta las dos	ahs-tah lahs dohs
before 3:00	antes de las tres	ahn-tehs deh lahs trehs
after 3:00	después de las tres	dehs-pwehs deh lahs trehs
since what time	desde qué hora	dehs-deh keh oh-rah
since 6:00	desde las seis	dehs-deh lahs seh-yees
an hour ago	hace una hora	ah-seh oo-nah oh-rah
per hour	por hora	pohr oh-rah
early	temprano	tehm-prah-noh
late	tarde	tahr-deh
late (in arriving)	en retraso	ehn rreh-trah-soh
on time	a tiempo	ah tee-yehm-poh
see you later	hasta luego	ahs-tah loo-weh-goh
see you soon	hasta la vista	ahs-tah lah bees-tah
see you tomorrow	hasta mañana	ahs-tah mah-nyah-nah
good-bye	adiós	ah-dee-yohs

Fast Forward

Look in your local newspaper and, in Spanish, read aloud the movie times for the films you want to see.

Chapter 6

A Hospitable Hotel

In This Chapter

➤ Getting the best from your hotel

➤ Ordinal numbers

No matter where you go in the Spanish-speaking world, a U.S. travel agent can help you find accommodations and make reservations that suit both your needs and your budget. For the more adventurous traveler, it might prove more economical to bargain for a room rate in Mexico or in rural areas throughout the Spanish-speaking world. You can expect to find the following types of lodgings in your travels, especially in Spain.

What a Place! Does It Have . . .?

Before leaving home, you probably should check with your travel agent or the hotel's management to make sure the hotel you've chosen has the amenities you desire.

Depending on your requirements, you need to know the words for everything from bathroom to swimming pool. Even with reservations, you'll end up with some surprises—but it never hurts to ask questions when you are making arrangements. See Table 6.1 for a basic list of hotel amenities.

Is (Are) there . . .?
¿Hay . . .?
Ahy

Table 6.1 Hotel Facilities

Term	Spanish	Pronunciation
a bar	un bar	oon bahr
a bellman	un portero	oon pohr-teh-roh
a business center	un centro de negocios	oon sehn-troh deh neh-goh-see-yohs
a concierge (caretaker)	un conserje	oon koh-sehr-heh
a doorman	un portero	oon pohr-teh-roh
an elevator	un ascensor	oon ah-sehn-sohr
a fitness center	un gimnasio	oon heem-nah-see-yoh
a gift shop	una tienda de regalos	oo-nah tee-yehn-dah deh rreh-gah-lohs
a laundry and dry cleaning service	una lavandería	oo-nah lah-bahn-deh-ree-yah
maid service	una gobernanta	oo-nah goh-behr-nahn-tah
a restaurant	un restaurante	oon rrehs-tow-rahn-teh
a staircase	una escalera	oo-nah ehs-kah-leh-rah
a swimming pool	una piscina	oo-nah pee-see-nah
valet parking	una atendencia del garaje	oo-nah ah-tehn-dehn-see-yah dehl gah-rah-heh

¡Cuidado!

In Spanish buildings, the ground floor is called la planta baja (lah plahn-tah bah-hah), which literally means "the lower floor." The basement is called el sótano (ehl soh-tah-noh). Expect to see the abbreviations PB and Sót. for these levels on elevator buttons. The word piso (pee-soh) refers to floors above ground level.

Getting What You Want

Is something missing? Are you dissatisfied with your accommodations? If you need something to make your stay more enjoyable, don't be afraid to speak up. Table 6.2 lists a few items you might want or need.

I would like . . .	Please send me . . .
Quisiera . . .	Haga el favor de mandarme . . .
kee-see-yeh-rah	hah-gah ehl fah-bohr deh mahn-dahr-meh
I need . . .	There isn't (aren't) . . .
Me falta(n) . . .	No hay . . .
meh fahl-tah(n)	noh ahy
I need . . .	
Necesito . . .	
neh-seh-see-toh	

Table 6.2 Wants and Needs

Phrase	Spanish	Pronunciation
air conditioning	aire acondicionado	ahy-reh ah-kohn-dee-syoh-nah-doh
an alarm clock	un despertador	oon dehs-pehr-tah-dohr
an ashtray	un cenicero	oon seh-nee-seh-roh
a balcony	un balcón	oon bahl-kohn
a bar of soap	una pastilla de jabón	oo-nah pahs-tee-yah deh hah-bohn
a bathroom (private)	un baño privado	oon bah-nyoh pree-bah-doh
a bellhop	un botones	oon boh-toh-nehs
a blanket	una manta	oo-nah mahn-tah
a chambermaid	una camarera	oo-nah kah-mah-reh-rah
a hair dryer	un secador de pelo	oon seh-kah-dohr deh peh-loh
hangers	unas perchas	oo-nahs pehr-chahs
ice cubes	cubitos de hielo	koo-bee-tohs deh yeh-loh
a key	una llave	oo-nah yah-beh
mineral water	agua mineral	ah-gwah mee-neh-rahl
on the courtyard	con vista al patio	kohn bees-tah ahl pah-tee-yoh
on the garden	con vista al jardín	kohn bees-tah ahl har-deen
on the sea	con vista al mar	kohn bees-tah ahl mahr
a pillow	una almohada	oo-nah ahl-moh-hah-dah
a roll of toilet paper	un rollo de papel higiénico	oon rroh-yoh deh pah-pehl ee-zhee-yeh-nee-koh
a room	una habitación	oo-nah ah-bee-tah-see-yohn
a safe (deposit box)	una caja fuerte	oo-nah kah-hah fwehr-teh
a shower	una ducha	oo-nah doo-chah

Phrase	Spanish	Pronunciation
single (double) room	una habitación con una sola cama (con dos camas)	oo-nah ah-bee-tah-see-yohn kohn oo-nah soh-lah kah-mah (kohn dohs kah-mahs)
a telephone (dial-direct)	un teléfono (directo)	oon teh-leh-foh-noh dee-rehk-toh
a television (color)	una televisión (en color)	oo-nah teh-leh-bee-see-yohn (ehn koh-lohr)
tissues	pañuelos de papel	pah-nyoo-weh-lohs deh pah-pehl
toilet facilities	un W.C.	oon doh-bleh-beh seh
a towel	una toalla	oo-nah toh-wah-yah
a transformer (an electric adaptor)	un transformador	oon trahns-fohr-mah-dohr

Bathroom Etiquette

In many foreign countries, especially in older establishments, the sink and bathtub (and/or shower) are located in what is called the bathroom—el baño (ehl bah-nyoh)—while the toilet and bidet are in the water closet—the W.C (ehl doh-bleh-beh seh). Showers are often of the hand-held type and are not affixed to the wall, which sometimes makes them rather difficult to negotiate. A bidet is a marvelous accessory that can be found in many foreign countries. It allows a person to clean his or her private parts in a very discreet way. The user must face forward, straddle the bidet, and manually turn on controlled jets of hot and cold water. Please use it properly. It is not for feet or dirty laundry.

Something Extra

Don't forget to show good manners by using the following phrases:

Por favor.	De nada.	Muchas gracias.
pohr fah–bohr	deh nah–dah	moo-chahs
Please.	You're welcome.	grah-see-yahs
		Thank you.

When There's a Problem

Upon arrival, it is not uncommon to find that your room isn't exactly what you expected. Use the following phrases when you have a problem:

I don't like the room.
No me gusta la
habitación.
noh meh goos-tah lah
ah-bee-tah-see-yohn

Do you have something . . .?
¿Hay algo . . .?
ahy ahl-goh . . .

better
mejor
meh-hohr

cheaper
más barato
mahs bah-rah-toh

bigger
más grande
mahs grahn-deh

quieter
más privado
mahs pree-bah-doh

smaller
más pequeño
mahs peh-keh-nyoh

¿Would you please put another bed in the room?
¿Podría poner otra cama en la habitación, por favor?
poh-dree-yah poh-nehr oh-trah kah-mah ehn lah
ah-bee-tah-see-yohn pohr fah-bohr

. . . doesn't work.
. . . no funciona.
. . . noh foonk-see-yoh-nah

Can you fix it as soon as possible?
¿Puede arreglarlo lo más pronto posible?
pweh-deh ah-rreh-glahr-loh loh mahs prohn-toh
poh-see-bleh

How much is this room?
¿Cuánto cuesta esta habitación?
kwahn-toh kwehs-tah ehs-tah ah-bee-tah-see-yohn

Up, Up, and Away

We've all had an elevator experience—either in a hotel or
elsewhere—in which we've felt like a large sardine in a
small can. When you're pushed to the back or squished to
the side, you have to hope that a kind and gentle soul will
wiggle a hand free and ask, "¿Qué piso, por favor (keh
pee-soh pohr fah-bohr)?" You will need the ordinal numbers in Table 6.3 to give a correct answer, such as "El
segundo piso, por favor (ehl seh-goon-doh pee-soh pohr
fah-bohr)."

Table 6.3   Ordinal Numbers

No.	Spanish	Pronuncuation	No.	Spanish	Pronuncuation
1st	primero	pree-meh-roh	6th	sexto	sehks-toh
2nd	segundo	seh-goon-doh	7th	séptimo	sehp-tee-moh
3rd	tercero	tehr-seh-roh	8th	octavo	ohk-tah-boh
4th	cuarto	kwahr-toh	9th	noveno	noh-beh-noh
5th	quinto	keen-toh	10th	décimo	deh-see-moh

The Spanish ordinal numbers are abbreviated as follows:

primero 1° (or primer 1ᵉʳ)   tercero 3° (or tercer 3ᵉʳ)

segundo 2°   cuarta 4ª

When using ordinal numbers, keep the following in mind:

➤ Change the final -o of the masculine form to -a to make ordinal numbers feminine.

el segundo acto   the second act

la segunda escena   the second scene

➤ In Spanish, only use ordinal numbers through the 10th. After that, cardinal numbers are used.

la primera persona   the first person

la Tercera Avenida   Third Avenue

la página treinta   page 30

¡Cuidado!

When a cardinal number is used as an ordinal number, it is always masculine because the word *número*, which is masculine, is understood.

la página doscientos
page 200

➤ The words *primero* and *tercero* drop their final -o before a masculine, singular noun.

el primer hombre   the first man

la primera mujer   the first woman

el tercer día	the third day
la tercera semana	the third week
BUT	
el siglo tercero	the third century

Fast Forward

Open a book you have handy. Look at the page number and state it in Spanish. Repeat this 10 times.

Chapter 7

It's a Beautiful Morning!

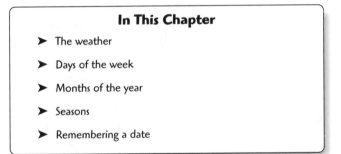

In This Chapter

➤ The weather

➤ Days of the week

➤ Months of the year

➤ Seasons

➤ Remembering a date

Whenever you plan a trip, you need to know what weather to anticipate so you can plan and pack properly. Remember that in South American countries below the Equator, the seasons are the opposite of what we experience here. And after you arrive in a country, you'll want to be able to read or listen to the weather forecast (el pronóstico, ehl proh-nohs-tee-koh) so you can arrange your sightseeing trips and outings accordingly. The phrases in Table 7.1 will help you with the weather.

Table 7.1   Weather Expressions

Expression	Spanish	Pronunciation
What's the weather?	¿Qué tiempo hace?	keh tee-yehm-poh ah-seh
It's beautiful.	Hace buen tiempo.	ah-seh bwehn tee-yehm-poh
It's hot.	Hace calor.	ah-seh kah-lohr
It's sunny.	Hace sol.	ah-seh sohl
It's nasty (bad).	Hace mal tiempo.	ah-seh mahl tee-yehm-poh
It's cold.	Hace frío.	ah-seh free-yoh
It's cool.	Hace fresco.	ah-seh frehs-koh
It's windy.	Hace viento.	ah-seh bee-yehn-toh
It's lightning.	Hay relámpagos.	ah-ee rreh-lahm-pah-gohs
It's thundering.	Truena.	troo-weh-nah
It's foggy.	Hay niebla. Hay neblina.	ahy nee-eh-blah ahy neh-blee-nah
It's humid.	Hay humedad.	ahy oo-meh-dahd
It's cloudy.	Hay nubes. Está nublado.	ahy noo-behs ehs-tah noo-blah-doh
It's overcast.	Está cubierto.	ehs-tah koo-bee-yehr-toh
It's raining.	Llueve. Está lloviendo.	yoo-weh-beh ehs-tah yoh-bee-yehn-doh
It's pouring.	Hay llovias torrenciales.	ah-ee yoh-bee-yahs toh-rrehn-see-yahl-ehs
It's snowing.	Nieva. Está nevando.	nee-eh-bah ehs-tah neh-bahn-doh
There'a a windstorm.	Hay un vendaval.	ahy oon behn-dah-vahl
There's hail.	Hay granizo.	ahy grah-nee-soh
There are showers.	Hay lloviznas.	ahy yoh-bees-nahs

Baby, It's Hot Outside!

It's not this simple in Spanish-speaking countries. Why?
They use the Celsius scale rather than the Fahrenheit scale

to which we are accustomed. This means that when the concierge tells you it's 20 degrees (Celsius), it's really a pleasant 68 degrees Fahrenheit. To ask for the temperature, simple say:

What's the temperature?
¿Cuál es la temperatura?
kwahl ehs lah tehm-peh-rah-too-rah

It's 50 degrees.
Hay una temperatura de cincuenta grados.
ahy oo-nah tehm-peh-rah-too-rah deh seen-kwehn-tah grah-dos

It's zero degrees.
Hay una temperatura de cero.
ahy oo-nah tehm-peh-rah-too-rah deh seh-roh

It's two degrees below zero.
Hay una temperatura de menos dos grados.
ahy oo-nah tehm-peh-rah-too-rah deh meh-nohs dohs grah-dos

Fast Forward

Look at the weather map in your daily newspaper. Give the weather and temperature in Spanish for cities throughout the country.

Something Extra

To convert Fahrenheit to Celsius (Centigrade), subtract 32 from the Fahrenheit temperature and multiply the remaining number by 5/9. This gives you the temperature in degrees Centigrade.

To convert Centigrade to Fahrenheit, multiply the Centigrade temperature by 9/5 and then add 32. This gives you the temperature in degrees Fahrenheit.

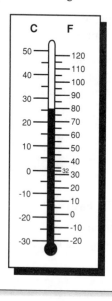

What Day Is It?

The more preoccupied you are or the busier you get, the more likely you are to forget the day of the week. When traveling, it's very important to keep track of your days so you don't wind up at a tourist attraction you absolutely had to see on the day it is closed. Study the days of the week in Table 7.2 so you don't miss a thing.

In Spanish, only capitalize days of the week when they are at the beginning of a sentence. When used elsewhere, unlike in English, they are written with a lowercase first letter.

| Sábado es un día. | Voy al supermercado el sábado. |
| Saturday is a day. | I go to the supermarket on Saturday. |

Something Extra

To express "on" when talking about a certain day, the Spanish use the definite article el.

> Voy al cine el viernes.
> I go to the movies on Friday(s).

Table 7.2   Days of the Week

Day	Spanish	Pronunciation
Monday	lunes	loo-nehs
Tuesday	martes	mahr-tehs
Wednesday	miércoles	mee-yehr-koh-lehs
Thursday	jueves	hoo-weh-behs
Friday	viernes	bee-yehr-nehs
Saturday	sábado	sah-bah-doh
Sunday	domingo	doh-meen-goh

¡Cuidado!

Unlike our calendars, Spanish calendars start with Monday. Don't let this confuse you when you give a quick glance. Make sure you get where you're going on the right day.

My Favorite Month

As you glance through glossy vacation brochures, you want to be able to figure out the best time to take your trip. Table 7.3 gives you the names of the months so you don't wind up in the wrong place at the wrong time.

Table 7.3 Months of the Year

Month	Spanish	Pronunciation
January	enero	eh-neh-roh
February	febrero	feh-breh-roh
March	marzo	mahr-soh
April	abril	ah-breel
May	mayo	mah-yoh
June	junio	hoo-nee-yoh
July	julio	hoo-lee-yoh
August	agosto	ah-gohs-toh
September	septiembre	sehp-tee-yehm-breh
October	octubre	ohk-too-breh
November	noviembre	noh-bee-yehm-breh
December	diciembre	dee-see-yehm-breh

Unless used at the beginning of a sentence, the names of all months should be written all lowercase.

Enero es un mes.   Voy a España en enero.
January is a month.   I go to Spain in January.

To Every Season Turn, Turn, Turn

Some seasons are better than others for traveling in certain countries. Make sure to plan your trip for when the weather will be great so you don't have to worry about hurricanes, storms, or other adverse conditions. Table 7.4 provides the names of the seasons.

Table 7.4   The Seasons

Season	Spanish	Pronunciation
winter	el invierno	ehl een-bee-yehr-noh
spring	la primavera	lah pree-mah-beh-rah
summer	el verano	ehl beh-rah-noh
autumn, fall	el otoño	ehl oh-toh-nyoh

When's Our Date?

No doubt, when making travel plans and arrangements, you often will have to refer to and ask for dates. Ask the following questions when you need information about the day and the date:

What day is it (today)?   What is today's date?
¿Qué día es (hoy)?   ¿A cuántos estamos hoy?
keh dee-yah ehs (oy)   ah kwahn-tohs
                        ehs-tah-mohs oy

What is (today's) the date?
¿Cuál es la fecha (de hoy)?
kwahl ehs lah feh-chah (deh oy)

The Spanish use the preposition en + the definite article for all seasons to express "in." Here's how it's done:

> Voy a México en el invierno, en la primavera, en el verano, y en el otoño.
> I go to Mexico in the winter, in the spring, in the summer, and in the fall.

You need to know how to express the date for appointments, travel plans, and meetings. In Spanish-speaking countries, the date is expressed as follows:

> day of week + el + (cardinal) number + de + month + de + year

> Hoy es sábado el nueve de mayo de mil novecientos noventa y ocho.
> Estamos a sábado el nueve de mayo de mil novecientos noventa y ocho.
> Today is Saturday, May 9, 1998.

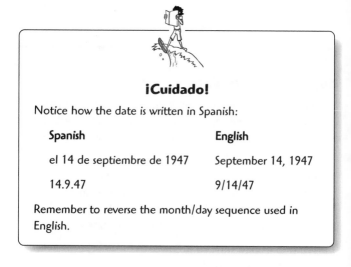

¡Cuidado!

Notice how the date is written in Spanish:

Spanish	English
el 14 de septiembre de 1947	September 14, 1947
14.9.47	9/14/47

Remember to reverse the month/day sequence used in English.

Use primero to express the first of each month.

el primero de mayo
May 1

BUT

el veinte y uno de mayo
May 21

el dos de mayo
May 2

Do not use hundreds, as we do in English, when giving the year.

mil novecientos noventa y nueve
1999

Use the definite article to express "on" with dates.

Me voy el once de julio.
I'm leaving on July 11.

Fast Forward

Give the dates of all the holidays you celebrate in Spanish. Then give the complete dates, including the year, for the most important events in your life.

Chapter 8

Sightseeing

Oooooh...

In This Chapter

➤ Sights for tourists

➤ How to make suggestions and plans

➤ How to give your opinion

When you travel to a foreign country, make sure to plan a logical itinerary of interesting sights to see. All the important tourist attractions you want to see for the day should be grouped in the same general vicinity. Running back and forth across a city will waste your precious vacation time. Always have a good game plan!

There's much to do and see in all the Spanish-speaking countries. Decide whether you are in the mood for sightseeing or for relaxing. Do you want to pack your day with activity or do you prefer to proceed at a leisurely pace? The brochures you've picked up at your hotel or at the tourist office will offer many suggestions.

Seeing the Sights

Whether you decide to go it alone or opt to take a tour, the following phrases will come in handy:

Where is there a tourist office?
¿Dónde hay una oficina de turismo?
dohn-deh ahy oo-nah oh-fee-see-nah deh too-rees-mah

What is there to see?
¿Qué hay a ver?
keh ahy ah behr

Where can I buy a map (a guide book)?
¿Dónde puedo comprar un mapa (una guía)?
dohn-deh pweh-doh kohm-prahr oon mah-pah
(oo-nah gee-yah)

At what time does it open (close)?
¿A qué hora se abre (se cierra)?
ah keh oh-rah seh ah-breh (seh see-yeh-rah)

What's the admission price?
¿Cuánto es la entrada?
kwahn-toh ehs lah ehn-trah-dah

Can children enter
for free?
¿Pueden entrar gratis
los niños?
pweh-dehn ehn-trahr
grah-tees lohs nee-nyohs

How much do they pay?
¿Cuánto pagan?
kwahn-toh pah-gahn

Until what age?
¿Hasta qué edad?
ahs-tah keh eh-dahd

Is it all right to take pictures?
¿Se puede sacar fotos?
seh pweh-deh sah-kahr
foh-tohs?

¡Cuidado!

If you see a sign saying "Prohibido Tomar Fotografías," no
picture taking is allowed.

I need a guide who
speaks English.
Necesito un guía de
habla inglés.
neh-seh-see-toh oon
gee-yah deh ah-blah
een-glehs

Where are there trips?
¿Dónde hay excursiones?
dohn-deh ahy ehks-
koor-see-yoh-nehs

How much does he (she) charge?
¿Cuánto cobra?
kwahn-toh koh-brah

May I Suggest . . .?

You've always had your heart set on seeing a bullfight.
The fascinating ads, posters, and pictures you've seen have
enticed you and have piqued your curiosity. You don't
know, however, how the others in your group feel about
accompanying you. Go for it! Make the suggestion. There
are several easy ways to do this.

Try asking this simple question:

¿Por qué no + nosotros form of the verb?
Why don't we...?

¿Por qué no vamos a una corrida de toros?
pohr keh noh bah-mohs ah oo-nah koh-rree-dah deh
toh-rohs
Why don't we go to a bullfight?

Try telling a friend what you'd like to do and then ask for his or her feelings about the idea.

> Quiero ir a una corrida de toros. ¿Qué crees (piensas)?
> kee-yeh-roh eer ah oo-nah koh-rree-dah deh toh-rohs
> keh kreh-yehs (pee-yehn-sahs)
> I want to go to a bullfight. What do you think?

Want to say let's? Use vamos a + the infinitive of the verb suggesting the activity.

> Vamos a ir a una corrida de toros.
> bah-mohs ah eer ah oo-nah koh-rree-dah deh toh-rohs
> Let's go to a bullfight.

Colloquially Speaking

If you're feeling rather confident with the language at this point, you might want to take a more colloquial approach to expressing yourself. You can use a number of phrases, all of which are followed by the infinitive of the verb. (The familiar tú forms are in parentheses.)

Phrase	Pronunciation	Meaning
¿Le (te) parece . . .?	leh (teh) pah-reh-seh	Do you want . . .?
¿Le (te) gustaría . . .?	leh (teh) goos-tah-ree-yah	Would you like . . .?
¿Tiene(s) ganas de . . .?	tee-yeh-neh(s) gah-hans deh	Do you feel like . . .?
¿Quiere(s) . . .?	kee-yeh-reh(s)	Do you want . . .?
¿Le (te) gustaría . . . ir al museo?		
¿Tiene(s) ganas de . . . ver una corrida de toros?		

Something Extra

All the preceding phrases can be made negative by adding no.

> ¿No le (te) parece . . .?
> Don't you want . . .?

Only petulant teenagers give abrupt yes or no answers to questions. Most of the rest of us say "Yes, but..." or "No, because..." If you'd like to elaborate on your answer, change the pronoun le or te from the question to me in your answer, as follows:

> Sí, me parece ir al museo.
> No, no me gustaría ir al museo.

Fast Forward

Pretend you are on a trip with a friend. Practice suggesting the things you would like to do.

So What Do You Think?

How do you feel about a suggestion made to you? Does the activity appeal to you? If so, you would say:

Me gusta el arte.
meh goos-tah ehl ahr-teh
I like art.

Me encanta la música.
meh ehn-kahn-tah lah
moo-see-kah
I adore music.

Soy aficionado(a) a la ópera.
soy ah-fee-see-yoh-nah-doh(dah) ah lah oh-peh-rah
I'm an opera fan.

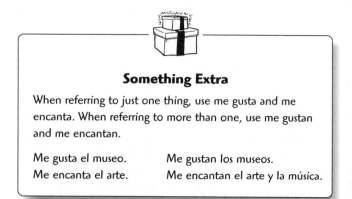

Something Extra

When referring to just one thing, use me gusta and me encanta. When referring to more than one, use me gustan and me encantan.

Me gusta el museo.	Me gustan los museos.
Me encanta el arte.	Me encantan el arte y la música.

When you do something or go somewhere new, different, exotic, or out of the ordinary, you're bound to have an opinion about whether you like it. Is it fun? Are you having a good time? Are you amused? Give your positive opinion by using Es (ehs, meaning "it is") + an adjective.

Adjective	Spanish	Pronunciation
awesome	bárbaro	bahr-bah-roh
excellent	excelente	ehk-seh-leh-teh
extraordinary	extraordinario	ehs-trah-ohr-dee-nah-ree-yoh
fabulous	fabuloso	fah-boo-loh-soh
fantastic	fantástico	fahn-tahs-tee-koh
fun	divertido	dee-behr-tee-doh
great	regio	rreh-hee-yoh
magnificent	magnífico	mag-nee-fee-koh
marvelous	maravilloso	mah-rah-bee-yoh-soh
out of this world	de película	deh peh-lee-koo-lah
phenomenal	fenomenal	feh-noh-meh-nahl

Adjective	Spanish	Pronunciation
sensational	sensacional	sehn-sah-see-yoh-nahl
stupendous	estupendo	ehs-too-pehn-doh
terrific	terrífico	teh-rree-fee-koh

Perhaps you don't like the suggestion presented. Maybe the activity bores you. To express your dislike, you might say:

Phrase	Spanish	Pronunciation
I don't like . . .	No me gusta . . .	noh meh goos-tah
I hate . . .	Odio, Detesto . . .	oh-dee-yoh, deh-tehs-toh
I'm not a fan of . . .	No soy aficionado(a) de . . .	noh soy ah-fee-see-yoh-nah-doh(dah) deh

To be a good sport, you tried the activity anyway. It was just as you thought—not your cup of tea. To give your negative opinion about an activity, you can use Es (ehs, meaning "it is") + an adjective.

Adjective	Spanish	Pronunciation
boring	aburrido	ah-boo-rree-doh
disagreeable	desagradable	deh-sah-grah-dah-bleh
a disaster	un desastre	oon deh-sahs-treh
horrible	horrible	oh-rree-bleh
a horror	un horror	oon oh-rohr
loathsome	asqueroso	ahs-keh-roh-soh
ridiculous	ridículo	rree-dee-koo-loh
silly	tonto	tohn-toh
terrible	terrible	teh-rree-bleh
ugly	feo	feh-yoh

Fast Forward

Open your local newspaper to the TV or movie listings.
Give your opinion in Spanish of the shows and films
currently available.

Chapter 9

The Shopping Experience

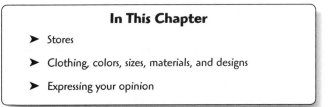

In This Chapter

➤ Stores

➤ Clothing, colors, sizes, materials, and designs

➤ Expressing your opinion

Are you particular about what you buy? Is it important to you to pick out the perfect gift or memento? Do you spend time agonizing over the right color, size, material, and design? Or is shopping such a chore that you choose almost anything you feel will be appropriate? Do you like to bargain? How about comparison shopping? No matter what your plan of action, shopping can be made a pleasant and enjoyable experience for everyone.

Do you prefer to browse in chic boutiques? Do you like to bargain in outdoor markets? Or are you attracted by a large, elegant mall (un centro comercial, oon sehn-troh koh-mehr-see-yahl)? Table 9.1 points you in the direction of stores that might interest you.

Table 9.1   Stores (Las Tiendas—lahs tee-yehn-dahs)

Store	Store
book store la librería lah lee-breh-ree-yah	newsstand el quiosco de periódicos ehl kee-yohs-koh deh peh-ree-yoh- dee-kohs
clothing store la tienda de ropa lah tee-yehn-dah deh rroh-pah	record store la tienda de discos lah tee-yehn-dah deh dees-kohs
department store el almacén ehl ahl-mah-sehn	souvenir shop la tienda de recuerdos lah tee-yehn-dah deh rreh-kwehr-dohs
florist la florería lah floh-reh-ree-yah	tobacco store la tabaquería lah tah-bah-keh-ree-yah
jewelry store la joyería lah hoh-yeh-ree-yah	toy store la juguetería lah hoo-geh-teh-ree-yah
leather goods store la marroquinería lah mah-rroh-keen-ree-yah	

¡Cuidado!

Remember to save your receipts when you make purchases in any foreign country. Foreign visitors are charged a value-added tax (VAT) on certain purchases. Some countries will return this tax (which could be considerable) upon presentation of a sales slip. Go to the specially marked windows at the airport or in large department stores to see whether any money is owed to you. Keep in mind that you also might have to pay U.S. taxes on your purchases.

If you are buying jewelry, you might want to ask the following questions:

¿Es macizo?
ehs mah-see-soh
Is it solid gold?

¿Es dorado?
ehs doh-rah-doh
Is it gold plated?

¿Es platino?
ehs plah-tee-noh
Is it platinum?

¿Es plata?
ehs plah-tah
Is it silver?

General Questions

Where can I find . . .?
¿Dónde se puede encontrar . . .?
dohn-deh seh pweh-deh ehn-kohn-trahr

Could you please help me?
¿Podría ayudarme, por favor?
poh-dree-yah ah-yoo-dahr-meh pohr fah-bohr

Would you please show me . . .?
¿Quiere enseñarme . . ., por favor?
kee-yeh-reh ehn-seh-nyahr-men pohr fah-bohr

Are there any sales?
¿Hay ventas (gangas)?
ahy behn-tahs (gahn-gahs)

Are there any discounts?
¿Hay rebajas (descuentos)
ahy rreh-bah-hahs (dehs-kwehn-tohs)

Do you sell . . .?
¿Vende . . .?
behn-deh

Where is (are) . . .?
¿Dónde está(n) . . .?
dohn-deh ehs-tah(n)

Do you have something . . .?
¿Tiene algo . . .?
tee-yeh-neh ahl-goh

Adjective	Spanish	Pronunciation
else	más	mahs
larger	más grande	mahs grahn-deh
smaller	más pequeño	mahs peh-keh-nyoh
longer	más largo	mahs lahr-goh
shorter	más corto	mahs kohr-toh
less expensive	más barato	mahs bah-rah-toh
more expensive	más caro	mahs kah-roh
better	de más alta calidad	deh mahs ahl-tah kah-lee-dahd

¿Does it come in another color?
¿Viene en otro color?
bee-yeh-neh ehn oh-troh koh-lohr

¿Can I try it on?
¿Puedo probarmelo?
pweh-doh proh-bahr-meh-loh

Can you alter it?
¿Puede arreglarlo?
pweh-deh ah-rreh-glahr-loh

Can I return it?
¿Puedo devolverlo?
pweh-doh deh-bohl-behr-loh

Will you wrap it please?
¿Quiere envolverlo, por favor?
kee-yeh-reh ehn-bohl-behr-loh pohr fah-bohr

Do you take credit cards?
¿Acepta tarjetas de crédito?
ahk-sehp-tah tahr-heh-tahs deh kreh-dee-toh

Do you take traveler's checks?
¿Acepta cheques de viajero?
ahk-sehp-tah cheh-kehs deh bee-yah-heh-roh

Clothing

It's always fun and interesting to buy an item of clothing in a foreign country. The styles and patterns are really quite unique and often prove to be a topic of conversation. Whether you decide to be daring and buy something native or you crave something at the height of fashion (a la última moda, ah lah ool-tee-mah moh-dah), Table 9.2 will help you in your quest.

Table 9.2 Clothing (La Ropa—lah roh-pah)

Item of Clothing	Spanish	Pronunciation
For One and All		
bathing suit	el traje de baño	ehl trah-heh deh bah-nyoh
belt	el cinturón	ehl seen-too-rohn
boots	las botas	lahs boh-tahs
gloves	los guantes	lohs gwahn-tehs
hat	el sombrero	ehl sohm-breh-roh
jacket	la chaqueta, el saco	lah chah-keh-tah, ehl sah-koh
jeans	los jeans, los vaqueros	lohs geens, lohs bah-keh-rohs
overcoat	el abrigo	ehl ah-bree-goh
pants	los pantalones	lohs pahn-tah-loh-nehs
pullover	el jersey	ehl hehr-see
raincoat	el impermeable	ehl eem-pehr-meh-yah-bleh
robe	la bata	lah bah-tah
sandals	las sandalias	lahs sahn-dah-lee-yahs
scarf	la bufanda	lah boo-fahn-dah
shirt (man-tailored)	la camisa	lah kah-mee-sah
shoes	los zapatos	lohs sah-pah-tohs
shorts	los pantalones cortos	lohs pahn-tah-loh-nehs kohr-tohs

continues

Table 9.2 **Continued**

Item of Clothing	Spanish	Pronunciation
sneakers	los tenis	lohs teh-nees
socks	los calcetines	lohs kahl-seh-tee-nehs
sweater	el suéter	ehl sweh-tehr
T-shirt	la camiseta, la playera	lah kah-mee-seh-tah, lah plah-yeh-rah
umbrella	el paraguas	ehl pah-rah-gwahs
underwear	la ropa interior	lah rroh-pah een-teh-ree-yohr
vest	el chaleco	ehl chah-leh-koh
For Men Only		
coat (sport)	el saco	ehl sah-koh
shorts (undergarments)	los calzoncillos	lohs kahl-sohn-see-yohs
suit	el traje	ehl trah-heh
tie	la corbata	lah kohr-bah-tah
undershirt	la camiseta	lah kah-mee-seh-tah
For Women Only		
bikini	el bikini	ehl bee-kee-nee
string	lah tohn-gah	la tonga
brassiere	el sostén	ehl sohs-tehn
blouse	la blusa	lah bloo-sah
dress	el vestido	ehl behs-tee-doh
negligee	el salto de cama	ehl sahl-toh deh kah-mah
panties	los pantaloncillos de mujer	lohs pahn-tah-lohn-see-yohs deh moo-hehr
pantyhose (tights)	las pantimedias	lahs pahn-tee-meh-dee-yahs
pocketbook	la bolsa	lah bohl-sah
skirt	la falda	lah fahl-dah
slip (half) (full)	el faldellín la combinación	ehl fahl-deh-yeen lah kohm-bee-nah-see-yohn
stockings	las medias	lahs meh-dee-yahs
suit	el traje sastre	ehl trah-heh sahs-treh

¡Cuidado!

Most countries use the metric system; therefore, their sizes are different from ours. Multiply by .39 to convert centimeters into inches. Multiply by 2.54 to convert inches into centimeters. The following conversion chart will help you get the size that's right for you.

CONVERSION TABLES FOR CLOTHING SIZES

WOMEN												
SHOES												
American	4	$4\frac{1}{2}$	5	$5\frac{1}{2}$	6	$6\frac{1}{2}$	7	$7\frac{1}{2}$	8	$8\frac{1}{2}$	9	$9\frac{1}{2}$	10
Continental	35	35	36	36	37	37	38	38	39	39	40	40	41

DRESSES, SUITS						
American	8	10	12	14	16	18
Continental	36	38	40	42	44	46

BLOUSES, SWEATERS						
American	32	34	36	38	40	42
Continental	40	42	44	46	48	50

MEN									
SHOES									
American	7	$7\frac{1}{2}$	8	$8\frac{1}{2}$	9	$9\frac{1}{2}$	10	$10\frac{1}{2}$	11	$11\frac{1}{2}$
Continental	39	40	41	42	43	43	44	44	45	45

SUITS, COATS							
American	34	36	38	40	42	44	46	48
Continental	44	46	48	50	52	54	56	58

SHIRTS							
American	14	$14\frac{1}{2}$	15	$15\frac{1}{2}$	16	$16\frac{1}{2}$	17	$17\frac{1}{2}$
Continental	36	37	38	39	40	41	42	43

Of course, you want to make sure you wind up with items that fit. Tell the salesperson the following:

I wear . . .	small	medium	large
Llevo el	pequeño	mediano	grande
tamaño . . .	peh-keh-nyoh	meh-dee-yah-noh	grahn-deh
yeh-boh ehl			
tah-mah-nyoh			

My size is . . .	small	medium	large
Mi talla es . . .	pequeña	mediana	grande
mee tah-yah	peh-keh-nyah	meh-dee-yah-nah	grahn-deh
ehs			

Colors

Do you see the world in primary colors? Or do you tend to go for the more exotic, artistic shades? Table 9.3 will help you learn the basic colors so you can get by.

Table 9.3 Colors (Los Colores—lohs koh-loh-rehs)

Color	Spanish	Pronunciation
beige	beige	beh-heh
black	negro	neh-groh
blue	azul	ah-sool
brown	pardo, marrón	pahr-doh, mah-rrohn
gray	gris	grees
green	verde	behr-deh
orange	anaranjado	ah-nah-rahn-hah-doh
pink	rosado	rroh-sah-doh
purple	morado	moh-rah-doh
red	rojo	rroh-hoh
white	blanco	blahn-koh
yellow	amarillo	ah-mah-ree-yoh

Something Extra

Add the word claro (klah-roh) to describe a color as light.
Add the word oscuro (oh-skoo-roh) to describe a color as dark.

| light green | dark blue |
| verde claro | azul oscuro |

Materials

While traveling, you might be tempted to make a clothing purchase. Do you find linen sexy? Do you love the feel of silk? Do you crave the coolness of cotton? Is leather a turn-on? Are you into wrinkle-free? We choose or reject different fabrics for a wide variety of reasons. Table 9.4 will help you pick the material you prefer for your special purchases. Use the word en (ehn) in when speaking about materials.

Table 9.4 Materials (Las Telas—lahs teh-lahs)

Material	Spanish	Pronunciation
cashmere	casimir	kah-see-meer
corduroy	pana	pah-nah
cotton	algodón	ahl-goh-don
denim	tela tejana	teh-lah teh-hah-nah
flannel	franela	frah-neh-lah
knit	tejido de punto	teh-hee-doh deh poon-toh
lace	encaje	ehn-kah-heh

continues

Table 9.4 Continued

Material	Spanish	Pronunciation
leather	cuero	kweh-roh
linen	hilo	ee-loh
nylon	nilón	nee-lohn
polyester	sintético	seen-teh-tee-koh
satin	raso	rrah-soh
silk	seda	seh-dah
suede	gamuza	gah-moo-sah
terry cloth	tela de toalla	teh-lah deh toh-wah-yah
velvet	terciopelo	tehr-see-yoh-peh-loh
wool	lana	lah-nah

Fast Forward

Open your closet. Label different articles of clothing. Each time you open the door, describe in Spanish one of the articles you have labeled. Make sure you give the color, size, material, and design.

Read the Labels

Have you ever accidentally washed a "Dry clean only" shirt? Have you ever washed a 100-percent cotton pair of jeans that could never be worn again? Make sure to read all labels carefully for the following information:

incontractable
lavable
een-koh-trahk-tah-bleh
lah-vah-bleh
non-shrinkable
washable

inarrugable
een-ah-rroo-gah-bleh
permanent press

Designs

Let's say you're on the hunt for a skirt like the ones worn by Spanish señoritas. Or maybe you'd like a plaid pair of golf pants because you really want to stand out. Or perhaps you're not even in the mood to shop, but you'd like to compliment someone on the good taste of his striped tie. Table 9.5 provides the words you need to describe patterns.

Table 9.5   Designs (Los Diseños— lohs dee-seh-nyohs)

Design	Spanish	Pronunciation
in a solid color	de color liso	deh koh-lohr lee-soh
with stripes	de rayas	deh rrah-yahs
with polka dots	de lunares	deh loo-nah-rehs
in plaid	de tartán	deh tahr-tahn
in herringbone	de espina depescado	deh ehs-pee-nah deh pehs-kah-doh
checked	de cuadros	deh kwah-drohs

Use a demonstrative adjective to express this, that, these, or those. Note that the adjective you choose depends upon the physical proximity of the noun to the subject.

Demonstrative Adjective	Masculine	Femimine
this	este (ehs-teh)	esta (ehs-tah)
these	estos (ehs-tohs)	estas (ehs-tahs)
that (near speaker)	ese (eh-seh)	esa (eh-sah)
those (near speaker)	esos (eh-sohs)	esas (eh-sahs)
that (far from speaker)	aquel (ah-kehl)	aquella (ah-keh-yah)
those (far from speaker)	aquellos (ah-keh-yohs)	aquellas (ah-keh-yahs)

Fast Forward

Open a magazine and comment on all the clothing you see. Give both positive and negative opinions.

Chapter 10

Food for Thought

In This Chapter

➤ Buying food

➤ How to express quantity

➤ How to order in a restaurant

➤ How to get the dish you want

➤ Special diets

Whether you stop by a local bodega or specialty store to grab a bite to tide you over or you make reservations in the fanciest of restaurants, you need to know how to ask for the foods you want and how to refuse those that don't have any appeal. You'll also want to make sure you order the proper quantity. This chapter will help you satisfy all your cravings.

Specialty Shops

Do you like to keep snacks in your hotel room, just in case you get the midnight munchies? Or have you rented a condo or an apartment and prefer to do your own cooking? In any Spanish-speaking country, you can enjoy the culinary delights that can be purchased in the shops listed in Table 10.1.

Table 10.1   Food Shops and What They Sell

En . . . (ehn, In . . .)	Yo compro . . . (yoh kohm-prah, I buy . . .)
grocery (vegetable) store la abacería lah ah-bah-seh-ree-yah	vegetables las legumbres lahs leh-goom brehs
	provisions las provisiones lahs proh-bee-see-yoh-nehs
butcher shop la carnicería lah kahr-nee-seh-ree-yah	meat la carne lah kahr-neh
bakery la panadería lah pah-nah-deh-ree-yah	desserts los postres lohs pohs-trehs
delicatessen la salchichonería lah sahl-chee-choh-neh-ree-yah	coldcuts los fiambres lohs fee-yahm-brehs
candy store la confitería lah kohn-fee-teh-ree-yah	candies los dulces lohs dool-sehs
dairy store la lechería lah leh-cheh-ree-yah	dairy products los productos lácteos lohs proh-dook-tohs lahk-teh-yohs
fruit store la frutería lah froo-teh-ree-yah	fruits las frutas lahs froo-tahs
pastry shop la pastelería lah pahs-teh-leh-ree-yah	pastry los pasteles lohs pahs-teh-lehs

En . . . (ehn, In . . .)	Yo compro . . . (yoh kohm-prah, I buy . . .)
fish store la pescadería lah pehs-kah-deh-ree-yah	fish el pescado ehl pehs-kah-doh
supermarket el supermercado ehl soo-pehr-mehr-kah-doh	provisions las provisiones lahs proh-bee-see-yoh-nehs
liquor store la tienda de licores lah tee-yehn-dah deh lee-koh-rehs	wines and liquors los vinos y licores lohs bee-nohs ee lee-koh-rehs

Something Extra

Many stores take their name from the product they sell, as follows:

pan	panadería
carne	carnicería
pastel	pastelería
leche	lechería
fruta	frutería
pescado	pescadería

There are many names for grocery stores throughout the Spanish-speaking world. Familiarize yourself with una tienda de comestibles, una tienda de abarrotes, una aborrotería, una pulpería, una tienda de ultramarinos, and una bodega. Be careful! In Spain, a bodega only sells wine from barrels. No food is available.

Food and More Food

Whether you're in a store or at a restaurant, knowing the Spanish names of the foods you like and dislike will put you at a distinct advantage. Use Tables 10.2 through 10.10 to pick and choose at will.

Table 10.2 Vegetables (Las Legumbres)

Vegetable	Spanish	Pronunciation
artichoke	la alcachofa	lah ahl-kah-choh-fah
asparagus	los espárragos	lohs ehs-pah-rah-gohs
beans (green)	las judías	lahs hoo-dee-yahs
beet	la remolacha	lah rreh-moh-lah-chah
broccoli	el brécol	ehl breh-kohl
carrot	la zanahoría	lah sah-nah-hoh-ree-yah
cauliflower	la coliflor	lah koh-lee-flohr
celery	el apio	ehl ah-pee-yoh
chickpeas	los garbanzos	lohs gahr-bahn-sohs
corn	el maíz	ehl mahy-ees
cucumber	el pepino	ehl peh-pee-noh
eggplant	la berenjena	lah beh-rehn-heh-nah
lettuce	la lechuga	lah leh-choo-gah
mushroom	el champiñon	ehl chahm-pee-nyohn
onion	la cebolla	lah seh-boh-lyah
peas	los guisantes	lohs gee-sahn-tehs
pepper	la pimienta	lah pee-mee-yehn-tah
potato	la papa, la patata	lah pah-pah, lah pah-tah-tah
rice	el arroz	ehl ah-rohs
spinach	la espinaca	lah ehs-pee-nah-kah
squash	la cucurbitácea	lah koo-koor-bee-tah-see-yah
sweet potato	la papa dulce	lah pah-pah dool-seh
tomato	el tomate	ehl toh-mah-teh
zucchini	el calabacín	ehl kah-lah-bah-seen

Table 10.3 Fruits (Las Frutas)

Fruit	Spanish	Pronunciation
apple	la manzana	lah mahn-sah-nah
apricot	el albaricoque	ehl ahl-bah-ree-koh-keh
banana (green)	la banana (el plátano)	lah bah-nah-nah (ehl plah-tah-noh)
blueberry	el mirtilo	ehl meer-tee-loh
cherry	la cereza	lah seh-reh-sah
coconut	el coco	ehl koh-koh
date	el dátil	ehl dah-teel
fig	el higo	ehl ee-goh
grape	la uva	lah oo-bah
grapefruit	el pomelo	ehl poh-meh-loh
lemon	el limón	ehl lee-mohn
lime	la lima	lah lee-mah
melon	el melón	ehl meh-lohn
olive	la aceituna	lah ah-seh-yee-too-nah
orange	la naranja	lah nah-rahn-hah
peach	el melocotín	ehl meh-loh-koh-teen
pear	la pera	lah peh-rah
pineapple	la piña	lah pee-nyah
plum	la ciruela	lah see-roo-weh-lah
prune	la ciruela pasa	lah see-roo-weh-lah pah-sah
raisin	la uva seca	lah oo-bah seh-kah
raspberry	la frambuesa, la mora	lah frahm-bweh-sah, lah moh-rah
strawberry	la fresa	lah freh-sah
tangerine	la mandarina	lah mahn-dah-ree-nah
watermelon	la sandía	lah sahn-dee-yah

Something Extra

Many tropical fruits that can be purchased in countries throughout the Hispanic world are rich in vitamins and minerals. The papaya is even said to have extraordinary medicinal qualities. If you are a fruit lover, you might want to try the following:

el aguacate	the avocado
la papaya	the papaya, a small melon-like fruit
la guayaba	the guava
el plátano	the plantain, a large green banana
el mamey	the mamey, a coconut-like fruit
el zapote	the zapote, an apple-shaped fruit with green skin and black pulp

Table 10.4   Meats (Las Carnes)

Meat	Spanish	Pronunciation
beef	la carne de vaca	lah kahr-neh deh bah-kah
chop, cutlet	la chuleta	lah choo-leh-tah
chopped meat	la carne picada	lah kahr-neh pee-kah-dah
filet mignon	el lomo fino	ehl loh-moh fee-noh
ham	el jamón	ehl hah-mohn
hamburger	la hamburguesa	lah ahm-boor-geh-sah
kidneys	los riñones	lohs rree-nyoh-nehs
lamb	la carne de cordero	lah kahr-neh deh kohr-deh-roh

Meat	Spanish	Pronunciation
liver	el hígado	ehl ee-gah-doh
pork	la carne de cerdo	lah kahr-neh deh sehr-doh
roast beef	el rosbíf	ehl rrohs-beef
sausage	la salchicha	lah sahl-chee-chah
steak	el bistec	ehl bees-tehk
stew	el estofado, el guisado	ehl ehs-toh-fah-doh, ehl gee-sah-doh
veal	la carne de ternera	lah kahr-neh deh tehr-neh-rah

Something Extra

Do you enjoy a nice, thick, meaty sandwich when you're really hungry? Why not try un sándwich cubano (oon sahn-weesh koo-bah-noh)? This Latin American treat is made from a long, crusty bread called pan de flauta (pahn day flow-tah), which translates literally as flute bread. The bread probably received this name because it is long and thin, similar to French and Italian bread. Slice the bread in half horizontally and add jamón (hah-mohn), ham; mortadela (mohr-tah-deh-lah), a meat similar to bologna; pierna de puerco (pee-yehr-nah deh pwehr-koh), pork; queso (keh-soh), cheese; pepinillos (peh-pee-nee-yohs), pickles; and salt, pepper, mayonnaise, and mustard according to taste. Heat this until the cheese melts. Is your mouth watering yet?

Table 10.5   Fowl and Game (La Carne Ave y de Caza)

Fowl or Game	Spanish	Pronunciation
chicken	el pollo	ehl poh-yoh
duck	el pato	ehl pah-toh
rabbit	el conejo	ehl koh-neh-hoh
turkey	el pavo	ehl pah-boh
venison	el venado	ehl beh-nah-doh

Table 10.6   Fish and Seafood (El Pescado y Los Mariscos)

Fish or Seafood	Spanish	Pronunciation
anchovy	la anchoa	la ahn-choh-ah
bass	la merluza	lah mehr-loo-sah
clam	la almeja	lah ahl-meh-hah
codfish	el bacalao	ehl bah-kah-lah-oh
crab	el cangrejo	ehl kahn-greh-hoh
flounder	el lenguado	ehl lehn-gwah-doh
grouper	el mero	ehl meh-roh
halibut	el halibut	ehl ah-lee-buht
herring	el arenque	ehl ah-rehn-keh
lobster	la langosta	lah lahn-gohs-tah
mackerel	la caballa	lah kah-bah-yah
monkfish	el rape	ehl rrah-peh
mussel	el mejillón	lah meh-hee-yohn
oyster	la ostra	lah ohs-trah
red snapper	el pargo colorado	ehl pahr-goh koh-loh-rah-doh
salmon	el salmón	ehl sahl-mohn
sardine	la sardina	lah sahr-dee-nah
scallops	las conchas de peregrino	lahs kohn-chahs deh peh-reh-gree-noh

Fish or Seafood	Spanish	Pronunciation
shrimp	los camarones, las gambas	lohs kah-mah-roh-nehs, lahs gahm-bahs
snails	los caracoles	lohs kah-rah-koh-lehs
sole	el lenguado	ehl lehn-gwah-doh
swordfish	el pez espada	ehl pehs ehs-pah-dah
trout	la trucha	lah troo-chah
tuna	el atún	ehl ah-toon

Table 10.7   Dairy Products (Productos Lácteos)

Dairy Product	Spanish	Pronunciation
butter	la mantequilla	lah mahn-teh-kee-yah
cheese	el queso	ehl keh-soh
cream	la crema	lah kreh-mah
eggs	los huevos	lohs hweh-bohs
yogurt	el yogur	ehl yoh-goohr

Table 10.8   Bakery Items (Pan y Postres)

Bread or Dessert	Spanish	Pronunciation
biscuit	el bizcocho	ehl bees-koh-choh
bread	el pan	ehl pahn
cake	el pastel	ehl pahs-tehl
cookie	la galleta	lah gah-yeh-tah
pie	el pastel	ehl pahs-tehl
rice pudding	el arroz con leche	ehl ah-rohs kohn leh-cheh
rolls (sweet)	los panecillos (dulces)	lohs pah-neh-see-yohs (dool-sehs)

Table 10.9 Sweet Things (Los Dulces)

Sweets	Spanish	Pronunciation
candy	los dulces	lohs dool-sehs
chocolate	el chocolate	ehl choh-koh-lah-teh
gum	el chicle	ehl chee-kleh

Table 10.10 Beverages (Las Bebidas)

Drink	Spanish	Pronunciation
beer	la cerveza	lah sehr-beh-sah
champagne	el champán	ehl chahm-pahn
cider	la sidra	lah see-drah
coffee (iced)	el café (helado)	ehl kah-feh (eh-lah-doh)
hot chocolate (cocoa)	el chocolate	ehl choh-koh-lah-teh
juice	el jugo	ehl hoo-goh
lemonade	la limonada	lah lee-moh-nah-dah
milk	la leche	lah leh-cheh
milk shake	el batido de leche	ehl bah-tee-doh deh leh-cheh
mineral water carbonated	el agua mineral con gas	ehl ah-gwah kohn gahs
non-carbonated	sin gas	seen gahs
orangeade	la naranjada	lah nah-rahn-hah-dah
soda	la gaseosa	lah gah-seh-yoh-sah
tea (iced)	el té (helado)	ehl teh (eh-lah-doh)
wine	el vino	ehl bee-noh

Fast Forward

Label all the food items in your refrigerator and kitchen cabinets.

Getting the Right Amount

In Spanish-speaking countries, the metric system is used when measuring quantities of food. Liquids are measured in liters, and solids are measured in kilograms or fractions thereof. Most of us are used to dealing with ounces, pounds, pints, quarts, and gallons. The following convenient conversion chart will help you out until the metric system becomes second nature.

Table 10.11 Measuring Quantities of Food*

U.S. Customary System	Metric Equivalent
Solid Measures	
1 oz.	28 grams
1/4 lb.	125 grams
1/2 lb.	250 grams
3/4 lb.	375 grams
1.1 lb.	500 grams
2.2 lb.	1000 grams (1 kilogram)
Liquid Measures	
1 oz.	30 milliliters
16 oz. (1 pint)	475 milliliters
32 oz. (1 quart)	950 milliliters (approximately 1 liter)
1 gallon	3.75 liters

*All weight and measurement comparisons are approximate

Not having been brought up on the metric system, I can understand that you still might be a little confused. The following table should make it even easier for you. Sometimes it's just simpler to ask for a box, bag, jar, and so on, and to commit to memory the amounts we're accustomed to—a pound, a quart, and so on. Consult Table 10.12 to easily get the amount you want or need.

Table 10.12   Getting the Amount You Want

Amount	Spanish	Pronunciation
a bag of	un saco de	oon sah-koh deh
a bar of	una tableta de	oo-nah tah-bleh-tah deh
a bottle of	una botella de	oo-nah boh-teh-yah deh
a box of	una caja de	oo-nah kah-hah deh
a bunch of	un atado de	oon ah-tah-doh deh
a can of	una lata de	oo-nah lah-tah deh
a dozen	una docena de	oo-nah doh-seh-nah deh
a half pound of	media libra de	meh-dee-yah lee-brah deh
a jar of	un pomo de	oon poh-moh deh
a package of	un paquete de	oon pah-keh-teh deh
a piece of	un pedazo de	oon peh-dah-soh deh
a pound of	una libra de	oo-nah lee-brah deh
a quart of	un litro de	oon lee-troh deh
a slice of	un trozo de	oon troh-soh deh

You really want to sample the dulce de zapote (dool-seh deh sah-poh-teh) that your Mexican cousin has prepared. You know the caloric content of the zapote pulp, orange juice, and sugar is high, but you long to savor its creamy texture and tangy flavor. Your cousin wants to give you more than just a taste. Here are some expressions that will help you limit the amount you receive.

Quantity	Spanish	Pronunciation
a little	un poco de	oon poh-koh deh
a lot	mucho(a)	moo-choh(chah)
enough	bastante, suficiente	bahs-tahn-teh, soo-fee-see-yehn-teh
too much	demasiado	deh-mah-see-yah-doh

Fast Forward

Write your weekly shopping list in Spanish. Include the quantities of the items you want to purchase.

It's Mealtime

Breakfast, el desayuno (ehl deh-sah-yoo-noh), is generally eaten between 7 a.m. and 9 a.m. in Spanish-speaking countries. It usually is much lighter than its American counterpart, consisting of coffee with milk and bread with butter or jam. Churros (fritters made by frying long strips of dough in oil and then sprinkling them with sugar) and chocolate (hot chocolate) are special favorites.

Regional snacks and drinks (batidas y licuados) that serve as midmorning snacks are consumed between 10:30 a.m. and noon.

Lunch, la comida in Spain and Mexico (lah koh-mee-dah) and el almuerzo in South America and the Caribbean (ehl ahl-mwehr-soh), is eaten between 1:30 p.m. and 3:30 p.m. and is considered the main meal of the day. It includes soup, meat or fish, vegetables, salad, and dessert.

La merienda (lah meh-ree-yehn-dah), a late afternoon snack, is generally served between 5:00 p.m. and 6:00 p.m. It customarily consists of coffee or tea and pastry.

Supper is referred to as la cena (lah seh-nah) in Spain and as la comida (lah koh-mee-dah) in Spanish America. This meals tends to be light because it is consumed late, sometimes after 9:00 p.m.

If you choose to dine in a restaurant, it might be necessary to reserve a table. When you call, make sure to include all the pertinent information, as follows:

I would like to reserve a table . . .
Quisiera hacer una reserva . . .
kee-see-yeh-rah ah-sehr oo-nah rreh-sehr-bah

for this evening.
para esta noche.
pah-rah ehs-tah noh-cheh

for tomorrow evening.
para mañana por la noche.
pah-rah mah-nyah-nah pohr lah noh-cheh

for Saturday evening.
para el sábado por la noche.
pah-rah ehl sah-bah-doh pohr lah noh-cheh

for two people.
para dos personas.
pah-rah dohs pehr-soh-nahs

for 8:30 p.m.
para las ocho y media.
pah-rah lahs oh-choh ee meh-dee-yah

on the terrace, please (outdoors).
en la terraza, por favor.
ehn lah teh-rrah-sah pohr-fah-bohr

in the corner.
en el rincón.
ehn ehl rreen-kohn

near the window.
cerca de la ventana.
sehr-kah deh lah behn-tah-nah

If you do not reserve a table and show up at a restaurant unannounced, el jefe de comedor (ehl heh-feh deh koh-meh-dohr), the head waiter, will surely ask the following:

A table for how many?
¿Una mesa para cuántas personas?
oo-nah meh-sah pah-rah kwahn-tahs pehr-soh-nahs

Make sure to answer his question completely, as follows:

A table for two, please.
Una mesa para dos, por favor.
oo-nah meh-sah pah-rah dohs pohr fah-bohr

At the Table

Let's say you've now been seated. You look around and are delighted with the fine china, the crystal, the linen napkins, and the crisp white table cloth. But wait! Your fork is missing and a glass is chipped. Table 10.13 provides the vocabulary you need when asking the waiter for cutlery or other missing pieces. Remember to say "Necesito..." (neh-seh-see-toh) to tell the waiter what you need.

Table 10.13 Tableware (Servicio de Mesa)

Tableware	Spanish	Pronunciation
bowl	un tazón	oon tah-sohn
cup	una taza	oo-nah tah-sah

continues

Table 10.13 Continued

Tableware	Spanish	Pronunciation
dinner plate	un plato	oon plah-toh
fork	un tenedor	oon teh-neh-dohr
glass	un vaso	oon bah-soh
knife	un cuchillo	oon koo-chee-yoh
menu	un menú	oon meh-noo
napkin	una servilleta	oo-nah sehr-bee-yeh-tah
place setting	un cubierto	oon koo-bee-yehr-toh
saucer	un platillo	oon plah-tee-yoh
soup dish	un sopero	oon soh-peh-roh
soup spoon	una cuchara	oo-nah koo-chah-rah
tablecloth	un mantel	oon mahn-tehl
teaspoon	una cucharita	oo-nah koo-chah-ree-tah
wine glass	una copa	oo-nah koh-pah

The waiter has come to give you a menu and to see whether you'd like a drink before dinner. You can use the following expressions for ordering both your food and drinks:

What is today's specialty?
¿Cuál es el plato del día de hoy?
kwahl ehs ehl plah-toh dehl dee-yah deh oy

What is the house specialty?
¿Cuál es la especialidad de la casa?
kwahl ehs lah ehs-peh-see-yah-lee-dahd deh lah kah-sah

What do you recommend?
¿Qué recomienda Ud.?
keh rreh-koh-mee-yehn-dah oo-stehd

I Need an Explanation

A Spanish menu can be confusing and overwhelming unless you know certain culinary terms. The waiter will probably get lost in his explanation. Table 10.14 gives you the terms you need to know.

Table 10.14 Understanding the Menu

Item	Pronunciation	Meaning
Sauces (Salsas)		
ají de queso	ah-hee deh keh-soh	cheese sauce
adobo	ah-doh-boh	chili sauce made with sesame seeds, nuts, and spices
mole	moh-leh	chili sauce made with sesame seeds, cocoa, and spices
pipían	pee-pee-yahn	chili and pumpkin seed sauce spiced with coriander and served with bread crumbs
salsa cruda	sahl-sah kroo-dah	an uncooked tomato sauce dip
salsa de tomatilla	sahl-sah deh toh mah-tee-yah	Mexican green tomato sauce
salsa de perejil	sahl-sah deh peh reh-heel	parsley sauce
verde	behr-deh	green chili and green tomato sauce
Chilies (Chiles)		
ancho	ahn-choh	medium hot
chipotle	chee-poh-tehl	hot, smokey flavored
jalapeño	hah-lah-peh-nyoh	hot, meaty flavored
pasilla	pah-see-yah	hot, rich, sweet flavored
pequín	peh-keen	hot
pimiento	pee-mee-yehn-toh	peppery
poblano	poh-blah-noh	medium hot, rich flavored
serrano	seh-rrah-noh	hot

continues

Table 10.14   Continued

Item	Pronunciation	Meaning
Tortillas (Tortillas)		
burrito	boo-ree-toh	flour tortilla with a cheese and meat filling served with salsa
chalupas	chah-loo-pahs	cheese or ground pork filled tortillas served with a green chili sauce
chilaquiles	chee-lah-kee-lehs	baked layers of tortillas filled alternately with beans, meat, chicken, and cheese
enchiladas	ehn-chee-lah-dahs	soft corn tortillas filled with meat, rice, and cheese and topped with spicy sauce
flautas	flow-tahs	rolled, flute-shaped, deep-fried tortilla sandwiches
quesadillas	keh-sah-dee-yahs	deep-fried tortillas covered with cheese, tomato, and pepper
tacos	tah-kohs	crisp toasted tortillas filled with meat, poultry, or beans and topped with shredded lettuce, cheese, and sauce
tostada	tohs-tah-dah	tortilla chip with different pepper and cheese toppings
Appetizers (Los Aperetivos)		
alcachofas	ahl-kah-choh-fahs	artichokes
almejas	ahl-meh-hahs	clams
anguilas ahumadas	ahn-gee-lahs ah-oo-mah-dahs	smoked eels
calamares	kah-lah-mah-rehs	squid
camarones	kah-mah-roh-nehs	shrimp
caracoles	kah-rah-koh-lehs	snails
champiñones	chahm-pee-nyoh-nehs	mushrooms
chorizo	choh-ree-soh	spicy sausage

Item	Pronunciation	Meaning
cigales	see-gah-lehs	crayfish
guacamole	gwah-kah-moh-leh	avocado spread
huevos	hweh-bohs	eggs
melón	meh-lohn	melon
moluscos	moh-loos-kohs	mussels
ostras	ohs-trahs	oysters
sardinas	sahr-dee-nahs	sardines
tostadas	tohs-tah-dahs	tortilla chips

Soups (Las Sopas)

gazpacho	gahs-pah-choh	puréed uncooked vegetables, served cold
potaje madrileño	poh-tah-heh mah-dree-leh-nyoh	thick, puréed cod, spinach, and chickpeas
sopa de ajo	soh-pah deh ah-hoh	garlic soup
sopa de albóndigas	soh-pah deh ahl-bohn-dee-gahs	meatball soup
sopa de cebolla	soh-pah deh seh-boh-lah	onion soup
sopa de fideos	soh-pah deh fee-deh-yohs	noodle soup
sopa de gambas	soh-pah deh gahm-bahs	shrimp soup
sopa de mariscos	soh-pah deh mah-rees-kohs	seafood soup
sopa de pescado	soh-pah deh pehs-kah-doh	fish soup
sopa de verduras	soh-pah deh behr-doo-rahs	soup made from puréed green vegetables

Proper Preparation

Of course, you want to make sure your meal is cooked just the way you like it. The waiter may ask the following:

> How do you want it (them)?
> ¿Cómo lo (los, la, las) quiere?
> koh-moh loh (lohs, lah, lahs) kee-yeh-reh

Table 10.15 will help you express your wants and needs.

Table 10.15   Preparing It Properly

Term	Spanish	Pronunciation
baked	asado	ah-sah-doh
boiled	hervido	ehr-bee-doh
breaded	empanado	ehm-pah-nah-doh
broiled	a la parrilla	ah lah pah-rree-yah
browned	al horno	ahl ohr-noh
chopped	picado	pee-kah-doh
fried	frito	free-toh
fried, deep fried	a la romana	ah lah rroh-mah-nah
grilled	asado a la parrilla	ah-sah-doh ah lah pah-rree-yah
in its juices	en su jugo	ehn soo oo-goh
marinated	escabechado	ehs-kah-beh-chah-doh
mashed	puré	poo-reh
poached	escalfado	ehs-kahl-fah-doh
pureed	puré	poo-reh
roasted	asado	ah-sah-doh
with sauce	con salsa	kohn sahl-sah
sautéed	salteado	sahl-teh-yah-doh
smoked	ahumado	ah-oo-mah-doh
steamed	al vapor	ahl bah-pohr
stewed	estofado	ehs-toh-fah-doh

Term	Spanish	Pronunciation
very rare	casi crudo	kah-see-kroo-doh
rare	poco asado	poh-koh ah-sah-doh
medium rare	un poco rojo pero no crudo	oon poh-koh rroh-hoh peh-roh noh kroo-doh
medium	a término medio	ah tehr-mee-noh meh-dee-yoh
well-done	bien asado (hecho, cocido)	byehn ah-sah-doh (eh-choh, koh-see-doh)
Eggs (Los Huevos) (lohs weh-bohs)		
fried	fritos	free-tohs
hard-boiled	duros	doo-rohs
poached	escalfados	ehs-kahl-fah-dohs
scrambled	revueltos	rreh-bwehl-tohs
soft-boiled	pasados por agua	pah-sah-dohs pohr ah-gwah
omelet	una tortilla	oo-nah tohr-tee-yah
plain omelet	una tortilla a la francesa	oo-nah tohr-tee-yah ah lah frahn-seh-sah
herb omelet	una tortilla con hierbas	oo-nah tohr-tee-yah kohn yehr-bahs

Spice It Up

Different spices are used in Spain and in the Spanish
American countries. Depend on menu descriptions or
your server to help you determine whether the dish will
be to your liking—bland or spicy. Table 10.16 will help
you with the spices you might encounter.

Table 10.16 Herbs, Spices, and Condiments (Hierbas, Especias, y Condimentos)

Term	Spanish	Pronunciation
basil	la albahaca	lah ahl-bah-ah-kah
bay leaf	la hoja de laurel	lah oh-hah deh low-rehl
butter	la mantequilla	lah mahn-teh-kee-yeh
caper	el alcaparrón	ehl ahl-kah-pah-rrohn
chives	el cebollino	ehl seh-boh-yee-noh
dill	el eneldo	ehl eh-nehl-doh
garlic	el ajo	ehl ah-hoh
ginger	el jenjibre	ehl hehn-hee-breh
honey	la miel	lah mee-yehl
jam, jelly	la mermelada	lah mehr-meh-lah-dah
ketchup	la salsa de tomate	lah sahl-sah deh toh-mah-teh
lemon	el limón	ehl lee-mohn
mayonnaise	la mayonesa	lah meh-yoh-neh-sah
mint	la menta	lah mehn-tah
mustard	la mostaza	lah mohs-tah-sah
nutmeg	la nuez moscada	lah nwehs mohs-kah-dah
oil	el aceite	ehl ah-seh-ee-teh
oregano	el orégano	ehl oh-reh-gah-noh
paprika	el pimentón dulce	ehl pee-mehn-tohn dool-seh
parsley	el perejil	ehl peh-reh-heel
pepper	la pimienta	lah pee-mee-yehn-tah
rosemary	el romero	ehl rroh-meh-roh
saffron	el azafrán	ehl ah-sah-frahn
salt	la sal	lah sahl
sesame	el ajonjolí	ehl ah-hohn-hoh-lee
sugar	el azúcar	ehl ah-soo-kahr
tarragon	el tarragón	ehl tah-rah-gohn

Term	Spanish	Pronunciation
thyme	el tomillo	ehl toh-mee-yoh
vinegar	el vinagre	ehl bee-nah-greh

¡Cuidado!

There is no Spanish word for "some" when the item can't be counted. Use Quisiera (kee-see-yeh-rah) + the noun to express what you want, as follows:

> Quisisera sal, por favor.
> I'd like some salt, please.

Special Requests

If you have certain likes, dislikes, or dietary restrictions that you would like to make known, keep the following phrases handy:

Phrase	Spanish	Pronunciation
I am on a diet.	Estoy a régimen.	ehs-toy ah rreh-hee-mehn
I'm a vegetarian.	Soy vegetariano(a).	soy beh-heh-tah-ree-yah-noh(nah)
I can't eat anything made with . . .	No puedo comer nada que contiene . . .	noh pweh-doh koh-mehr nah-dah keh kohn-tee-yeh-neh
I can't have . . .	No puedo tomar . . .	noh pweh-doh toh-mahr
any dairy products	productos lácteos	proh-dook-tohs lahk-teh-yohs

continues

continued

Phrase	Spanish	Pronunciation
any alcohol	alcohol	ahl-koh-ohl
any saturated fats	grasas saturadas	grah-sahs sah-too-rah-dahs
any shellfish	mariscos	mah-rees-kohs
I'm looking for a dish . . .	Estoy buscando un plato . . .	ehs-toy boos-kahn-doh oon plah-toh
high in fiber	con mucha fibra	kohn moo-chah fee-brah
low in cholesterol	con poco colesterol	kohn poh-koh koh-lehs-teh-rohl
low in fat	con poca grasa	kohn poh-kah grah-sah
low in sodium	con poca sal	kohn poh-kah sahl
non-dairy	non lácteo	nohn lahk-teh-yoh
salt-free	sin sal	seen sahl
sugar-free	sin azúcar	seen ah-soo-kahr
without artificial coloring	sin colorantes artificiales	seen koh-loh-rah-tehs ahr-tee-fee-see-yah-lehs
without preservatives	sin preservativos	seen preh-sehr-bah-tee-bohs

Please Take It Back to the Kitchen

At times, the cooking or the table setting might not be up to your standards. Table 10.17 presents some problems you might encounter.

Table 10.17   Possible Problems

Term	Spanish	Pronunciation
It's cold.	Está frío.	ehs-tah free-yoh
It's too rare.	Está demasiado crudo.	ehs-tah deh-mah-see-yah-doh kroo-doh

Term	Spanish	Pronunciation
It's over-cooked.	Está sobrecocido.	ehs-tah soh-breh-koh-see-doh
It's burned.	Está quemado.	ehs-tah keh-mah-doh
It's too salty.	Está muy salado.	ehs-tah mwee sah-lah-doh
It's too sweet.	Está muy azucarado.	ehs-tah mwee ah-soo-kah-rah-doh
It's too spicy.	Está demasiado picante.	ehs-tah deh-mah-see-yah-doh pee-kahn-teh
It's bitter (sour).	Está agrio (cortado).	ehs-tah ah-gree-yoh (kohr-tah-doh)
It tastes like . . .	Sabe a . . .	sah-beh ah
It's dirty.	Está sucio.	ehs-tah soo-see-yoh

Fancy Endings

When it's time for dessert, choose from among the delightful specialties in Table 10.18.

Table 10.18 Daring Desserts

Dessert	In Spanish	Pronunciation
caramel custard	el flan	ehl flahn
cookies	las galletas	lahs gah-yeh-tahs
gelatin	la gelatina	lah heh-lah-tee-nah
ice cream	el helado	ehl eh-lah-doh
pie	el pastel	ehl pahs-tehl
sponge cake	el bizcocho	ehl bees-koh-choh
tart	la tarta	lah tahr-tah
yogurt	el yogur	ehl yoh-goor

Make sure you get the ice cream you want for dessert.

cone	un barquillo	oon bahr-kee-yoh
cup	una copa	oo-nah koh-pah
chocolate	de chocolate	deh choh-koh-lah-teh
vanilla	de vainilla	deh bah-ee-nee-yah
strawberry	de fresa	deh freh-sah
pistachio	de pistacho	deh pees-tah-choh

The wines you might order include:

red wine	el vino tinto	ehl bee-noh teen-toh
rosé wine	el vino rosado	ehl bee-noh rroh-sah-doh
white wine	el vino blanco	ehl bee-noh blahn-koh
dry wine	el vino seco	ehl bee-noh seh-koh
sweet wine	el vino dulce	ehl bee-noh dool-seh
sparkling wine	el vino espumoso	ehl bee-noh ehs-poo-moh-soh
champagne	el champán	ehl chahm-pahn

Fast Forward

Go to a Spanish restaurant in your neighborhood. Order your meal in Spanish.

Chapter 11

How to Be a Social Butterfly

In This Chapter

➤ Amusements and diversions

➤ Invitations: extending, accepting, and refusing

Are you heading off to the sea to engage in water sports, up to the mountains for skiing or hiking, onto the links for a round of golf, or onto the courts for a brisk tennis match? Are you a film buff or a theatergoer? Do you enjoy a lively opera or an elegant ballet? Perhaps the game's the thing and you'll spend some time with a one-armed bandit in a luxurious casino. With the help of this chapter, you'll be able to do it all—as well as being a guest or doing the inviting.

I Live for Sports

Whether you like to relax as a beach bum, spend your days gazing out at the azure ocean, or feel compelled to engage in every fast-paced sport you can, you need certain words and terms to make your preferences known. Table 11.1 provides a list of sports and outdoor activities. The verbs hacer* and jugar + a + definite article** (el, la, los, las) are often used to show participation in a sport. Any verb indicated in parentheses is used in place of jugar or hacer.

I (don't) like . . .	I (don't) like . . .
(No) Me gusta . . .	(No) Me gustan . . .
(one sport)	(more than one sport)
(noh) meh goos-tah . . .	(noh) meh goos-than . . .

I want to play . . .
Quiero jugar + a + definite article . . .
kee-yeh-roh hoo-gahr (ah-sehr)

or

Quiero hacer . . .
Kee-yeh-roh ah-sehr

The verb querer is irregular and can be followed by the infinitive of a verb:

yo	quiero	kee-yeh-roh
tú	quieres	kee-yeh-rehs
él, ella, Ud.	quiere	kee-yeh-reh
nosotros	queremos	keh-reh-mohs
vosotros	queréis	keh-reh-ees
ellos, ellas, Uds.	quieren	kee-yeh-rehn

We want to play golf.
Nosotros queremos jugar al golf.
nohs-oh-trohs keh-reh-mohs hoo-gahr ahl gohlf

Table 11.1   Sports

Sport	Spanish	Pronunciation
aerobics	los aeróbicos*	lohs ah-yeh-roh-bee-kohs
baseball	el beísbol**	ehl beh-ees-bohl
basketball	el baloncesto** , el básquetbol**	ehl bah-lohn-sehs-toh, ehl bahs-keht-bohl
bicycling	el ciclismo * (montar a bicicleta)	ehl see-klees-moh (mohn-tahr ah bee-see-kleh-tah)
body-building	el culturismo*	ehl kool-too-rees-moh
fishing	la pesca (ir de pesca)	lah pehs-kah (eer deh pehs-kah)
golf	el golf**	ehl gohlf
horseback riding	la equitación*	lah eh-kee-tah-see-yohn
jai alai	el jai alai**	ehl ahy-lahy
jogging	el footing* (trotar)	ehl foo-teeng (troh-tahr)
sailing	la navegación* (navegar)	lah nah-beh-gah-see-yohn (nah-beh-gahr)
scuba (skin) diving	el buceo	ehl boo-seh-yoh
soccer	el fútbol**	ehl foot-bohl
surfing	el surf* (surfear)	ehl soorf (soor-feh-yahr)
swimming	la natación* (nadar)	lah nah-tah-see-yohn (nah-dahr)
tennis	el tenis**	ehl teh-nees
volleyball	el volíbol**	ehl boh-lee-bohl
water-skiing	el esquí acuático*	ehl ehs-kee ah-kwah-tee-koh

Something Extra

The verbs jugar* and hacer** are irregular:

Jugar	hoo-gahr	Hacer	ah-sehr
yo juego	hweh-goh	hago	ah-goh
tú juegas	hweh-gahs	haces	ah-sehs
él, ella, Ud. juega	hweh-gah	hace	ah-seh
nosotros jugamos	hoo-gah-mohs	hacemos	ah-seh-mohs
vosotros jugáis	hoo-gah-ees	hacéis	ah-seh-ees
ellos, ellas, Uds. juegan	hweh-gahn	hacen	ah-sehn

Fast Forward

Tell a friend which sports you like to participate in and which you prefer to watch on television.

Sports Equipment

You went on vacation but didn't trust the airlines with your golf clubs and tennis rackets. Or perhaps you thought you wouldn't want to play and now you've changed your mind. You can still have a good time and can enjoy your favorite sport if you borrow or rent equipment. Use the following phrases when you find yourself in a similar predicament.

I need . . .
Me falta(n) . . .
meh fahl-tah(n)
Necesito . . .
neh-seh-see-toh

Could you lend (rent) me . . .?
Podría Ud. prestarme
(alquilarme) . . .?
poh-dree-yah oo-stehd
prehs-tahr-meh
(ahl-kee-lahr-meh)

Please . . .
Por favor . . .
pohr fah-bohr

Table 11.2 Sports Equipment (El Equipo Deportivo)

Equipment	Spanish	Pronunciation
ball (football, soccer)	la bola	lah boh-lah
ball (baseball, jai alai, tennis)	la pelota	lah peh-loh-tah
ball (basketball)	el balón	ehl bah-lohn
bat	el bate	ehl bah-teh
bicycle	la bicicleta	lah bee-see-kleh-tah
boat	el barco	ehl bahr-koh
canoe	la canoa	lah kah-noh-wah
diving suit	la escafandra	lah ehs-kah-fahn-drah
fishing rod	la caña de pesca	lah kah-nyah deh pehs-kah
flippers	las aletas	lahs ah-leh-tahs
goggles	las gafas	lahs gah-fahs
golf clubs	los palos de golf	lohs pah-lohs deh gohlf
helmet diver's	el casco el yelmo	ehl kahs-koh ehl yehl-moh
mitt	el guante	ehl gwah-teh
net	la red	lah rrehd
racquet	la raqueta	lah rrah-keh-tah
skates	los patines	lohs pah-tee-nehs
skis	los esquis	lohs ehs-kees
surfboard	el acuaplano	ehl ah-kwah-plah-noh

Other Amusements

Perhaps sports aren't part of your agenda. There are plenty of other activities you can pursue to have a good time. The phrases in Table 11.3 will give you the tools to make

Table 11.3   Places to Go and Things to Do

El Lugar ehl loo-gahr	Pronunciation	The Place
ir a la opera	eer a lah oh-peh-rah	go to the opera
ir a la playa	eer ah lah plah-yah	go to the pool
ir a una discoteca	eer ah oo-nah dees-koh-teh-kah	go to a disco
ir a un ballet	eer ah oon bah-leht	go to a ballet
ir a un casino	eer ah oon kah-see-noh	go to a casino
ir al centro comercial	eer al sehn-troh koh-mehr-see-yahl	go to the mall
ir al cine	eer al see-neh	go to the movies
ir a un concierto	eer ah oon kohn-see-yehr-toh	go to a concert
ir al teatro	eer al teh- yah-troh	go to the theater
ir de excursión	eer deh ehks-koor-see-yohn	go on an excursion
quedarse en su habitación, casa	keh-dahr-seh ehn soo ah-bee- tah-see-yohn, kah-sah	stay in one's room, home

many other intriguing suggestions. Should you delight in going to the opera, the ballet, the theater, or a concert, don't forget to bring along *los gemelos*, binoculars.

La Actividad lah ahk-tee-bee-dahd	Pronunciation	The Activity
escuachar a los cantadores	ehs-koo-chahr ah lohs kahn-tah-doh-rehs	listen to the singers
nadar	nah-dahr	swim
tomar sol	toh-mahr sohl	sunbathe
bailar	bahy-lahr	dance
ver a los bailadores	behr ah lohs bahy-lah-doh-rehs	see the dancers
jugar	hoo-gahr	play, gamble
mirar los escaparates	mee-rahr lohs ehs-kah-pah-rah-tehs	window shop
ver una película	behr oo-nah peh-lee-koo-lah	see a film
escuchar la orquesta	ehs-koo-chahr lah ohr-kehs-tah	listen to the orchestra
ver un drama	behr oon drah-mah	to see a play
ver los sitios	behr lohs see-tee-yohs	see the sights
jugar a los naipes	hoo-gahr ah lohs nahy -pehs	play cards
jugar a las damas	hoo-gahr ah lahs dah-mahs	play checkers
jugar al ajedrez	hoo-gahr ahl ah-heh-drehs	play chess
leer una novela	leh-yehr oo-nah noh-beh-lah	read a novel

At the Movies and on Television

Do you crave some quiet relaxation? Is the weather bad? Do you feel like getting away from everyone and everything? There's always a movie or the television. It seems that cable has invaded the planet and can accommodate anyone who needs a few carefree hours. If you want to be entertained, consult Table 11.4 for the possibilities.

What kind of film are they showing?
¿Qué tipo de película están pasando?
keh tee-poh deh peh-lee-koo-lah ehs-tahn pah-sahn-doh

What's on television?
¿Qué hay en la televisión?
keh ahy ehn lah teh-leh-bee-see-yohn

Table 11.4 Movies and Television Programs

Program Type	Spanish	Pronunciation
adventure film	una película de aventura	oo-nah peh-lee-koo-lah deh ah-behn-too-rah
cartoons	los dibujos animados	lohs dee-boo-hohs ah-nee-mah-dohs
comedy	una comedia	oo-nah koh-meh-dee-yah
game show	un juego	oon hweh-goh
horror movie	una película de horror	oo-nah peh-lee-koo-lah deh oh-rrohr
love story	una película de amor	oo-nah peh-lee-koo-lah deh ah-mohr
mystery	un misterio	oon mees-teh-ree-yoh
news	las noticias	lahs noh-tee-see-yahs
police story	una película policiaca	oo-nah peh-lee-koo-lah poh-lee-see-yah-kah
science-fiction film	una película de ciencia ficción	oo-nah peh-lee-koo-lah deh see-yehn-see-yah feek-see-yohn

Program Type	Spanish	Pronunciation
soap opera	una telenovela	oo-nah teh-leh-noh-beh-lah
spy movie	una película de espía	oo-nah peh-lee-koo-lah deh ehs-pee-yah
talk show	un programa de entrevistas	oon proh-grah-mah deh ehn-treh-bees-tahs
weather	el parte meteorológico, el pronóstico	ehl pahr-teh meh-teh-yoh-roh-loh-hee-koh, ehl proh-nohs-tee-koh

Refer to the following explanations when you choose a movie or theater:

Forbidden for those under 18 unless accompanied by an adult.
Prohibida para menores de 18 años (a menos de que este acompañado por un adulto).

You must be older than 13.
Mayores de 13 años.

Original version, subtitled.
Versión original.

Dubbed in Spanish.
Versión doblada (doh-blah-dah) al español.

Reduced rate.
Tarifa reducida.

If you prefer television, you might get hooked on a telenovela (teh-leh-noh-beh-lah), which literally translates as "a novel for television." These shows are similar to our American soap operas. The telenovela is generally shown five days or nights a week and runs for about a year, unlike its American counterpart which lasts for years. In Spanish-speaking households, watching these dramas is often a family affair. Generations sit in front of the television watching the villains receive their just desserts, the good guys get their rewards, and the loving couple walk off into the sunset.

So What Did You Think?

If you enjoy the program, you might say:

Phrase	Spanish	Pronunciation
I love it!	¡Me encanta!	meh ehn-kahn-tah
It's a good movie.	Es una buena película.	ehs oo-nah bweh-nah peh-lee-koo-lah
It's amusing!	¡Es divertida!	ehs dee-behr-tee-dah
It's great!	¡Es fantástica!	ehs fahn-tahs-tee-kah
It's moving!	¡Me toca!	meh toh-kah
It's original!	¡Es original!	ehs oh-ree-hee-nahl

If the show leaves something to be desired, try the following phrases:

Phrase	Spanish	Pronunciation
I hate it!	¡La odio!	lah oh-dee-yoh
It's a bad movie!	¡Es una mala película!	ehs oo-nah mah-lah peh-lee-koo-lah
It's a loser!	¡Es un desastre!	ehs oon deh-sahs-treh
It's garbage!	¡Es basura!	ehs bah-soo-rah
It's the same old thing!	¡Siempre es lo mismo!	see-yehm-preh ehs loh mees-moh
It's too violent!	¡Es demasiado violenta!	ehs deh-mah-see-yah-dah bee-yoh-lehn-tah

Fast Forward

Look in the movie and television section of your local newspaper. Give your opinion about the movies and shows currently available.

Invitations

It isn't much fun to play alone. Why not ask someone to join you? To extend an invitation, you can ask the following:

> Do you want to join me (us)?
> ¿Quiere (Quieres) acompañarme (acompañarnos)?
> kee-yeh-reh (kee-yeh-rehs) ah-kohm-pah-nyahr-meh
> (ah-kohm-pah-nyahr-nohs)

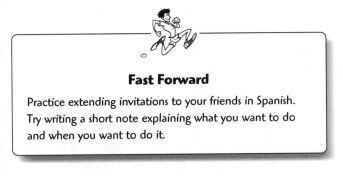

Fast Forward

Practice extending invitations to your friends in Spanish. Try writing a short note explaining what you want to do and when you want to do it.

Whether you've been invited to participate in a sport or an outing, to visit a museum, or just to stay at someone's home, the following phrases will allow you to graciously accept, to cordially refuse, or to show your indifference:

Phrase	Spanish	Pronunciation
Accepting		
Gladly.	Con placer.	kohn plah-sehr
Great!	¡Magnífico!	mahg-nee-fee-koh
If you want to.	Si tú quieres. (Ud. Quiere.)	see too kee-yeh-reh (oo-stehd kee-yeh-reh)
Okay. (I agree.)	De acuerdo.	deh ah-kwehr-doh
Of course.	Por supuesto.	pohr soo-pwehs-toh
That's a good idea.	Es una buena idea.	ehs oo-nan bweh-nah ee-deh-yah
Why not?	¿Por qué no?	pohr keh noh
With pleasure.	Con mucho gusto.	kohn moo-choh goos-toh
Refusing		
I'm busy.	Estoy ocupado.	ehs-toy oh-koo-pah-doh
I'm sorry.	Lo siento.	loh see-yehn-toh
I'm tired.	Estoy cansado.	ehs-toy kahn-sah-doh
I can't.	No puedo.	noh pweh-doh
I don't feel like it.	No tengo ganas.	noh tehn-goh gah-nahs
I don't want to.	No quiero.	noh kee-yeh-roh
Not again!	¿Otra vez?	oh-trah-behs
Showing Indifference		
I don't have any preference.	No tengo preferencia.	noh teh-goh preh-feh-rehn-see-yah
I don't know.	Yo no sé.	yoh noh seh
It depends.	Depende.	deh-peh-deh
Perhaps. Maybe.	Tal vez.	tahl behs
Whatever you want.	Lo que Ud. Prefiera (tú prefieras).	loh keh oo-stehd preh-fee-yeh-rah (too preh-fee-yeh-rahs)

Chapter 12

Personal Services

You've been traveling and having a wonderful time. All of a sudden you have a problem that just can't wait—your roots have surfaced in record time, you spilled tomato sauce on your new white silk shirt, you dropped your contact lens down the drain, you lost a heel on your shoe, or your four-year-old has dropped your camera in the bathtub. You're not home, and you're hesitant about what to do. Don't worry. You just have to know what to say to get the job done. Ask for las páginas amarillas (lahs pah-hee-nahs ah-mah-ree-yahs, the Yellow Pages), read the ads, and then explain your problem.

What a Bad Hair Day!

In the past, men went to a barbería (bahr-beh-ree-yah, a barber's) while women went to a salón de belleza (sah-lohn deh beh-yeh-sah, a beauty parlor). Today, these establishments have become more or less unisex, with men and women demanding more or less the same services. To get what you want simply ask:

Could you give me . . .   I would like . . .
Podría darme . . .   Quisiera . . .
poh-dree-yah dahr-meh . . .   kee-see-yeh-rah . . .

Today's salons provide the services listed in Table 12.1.

Table 12.1   Hair and Salon Care

Term	Spanish	Pronunciation
a haircut	un corte de pelo	oon kohr-teh deh peh-loh
a manicure	una manicura	oo-nah mah-nee-koo-rah
a pedicure	una pedicura	oo-nah peh-dee-koo-rah
a permanent	una permanente	oo-nah pehr-mah-nehn-teh
a rinse	un aclarado colorante	oon ah-klah-rah-doh koh-loh-rahn-teh
a set	un marcado	oon mahr-kah-doh
a shampoo	un champú	oon chahm-poo

Term	Spanish	Pronunciation
a trim	un recorte	oon rreh-kohr-teh
a waxing	una depilación	oo-nah deh-pee-lah-see-yohn
highlights	reflejos	rreh-fleh-hohs
layers	un corte en degradación	oon kohr-teh ehn deh-grah-dah-see-yohn

Do you need other services? Table 12.2 provides the phrases you need to get them. Use the following phrases to preface your request:

Could you please . . .
Podría Ud. . . . por favor
poh-dree-yah oo-stehd . . . poh fah-bohr

Table 12.2 Other Services

Service	Spanish	Pronunciation
blow dry my hair	secarme el pelo	seh-kahr-meh ehl peh-loh
curl my hair	rizarme el pelo	rree-sahr-meh ehl peh-loh
shave my beard my mustache my head	afeitarme la barba el bigote la cabeza	ah-feh-ee-tahr-meh lah bahr-bah ehl bee-goh-teh lah kah-beh-sah
straighten my hair	estirarme el pelo	ehs-tee-rahr-meh ehl peh-loh
trim my bangs	recortarme el flequillo	rreh-kohr-tahr-meh ehl fleh-kee-yoh
trim my beard (mustache, sideburns)	recortarme la barba (el bigote, las patillas)	rreh-kohr-tahr-meh lah bahr-bah (ehl bee-goh-teh lahs pah-tee-yahs)

Getting What You Want

It's hard enough getting the haircut and style you want when there is no language barrier—imagine the disasters that could befall your poor head in a foreign country! The following phrases will help make your styling and coloring preferences clear to your peinador (peh-nah-dor, hairstylist).

I prefer my hair . . .
Prefiero mi pelo . . .
preh-fee-yeh-roh mee peh-loh

I'd like a . . . style.
Quisiera un peinadeo . . .
kee-see-yeh-rah oon peh-ee-nah-doh

Style	Spanish	Pronunciation
long	largo	lahr-goh
medium	mediano	meh-dee-yah-noh
short	corto	kohr-toh
wavy	ondulado	ohn-doo-lah-doh
curly	rizado	rree-sah-doh
straight	lacio (liso)	lah-see-yoh (lee-soh)

Does your hair sometimes feel stiff as a board after a stylist has coated it with mousse, gel, or spray? How do you feel about all those chemicals going onto your head? Do you get allergic reactions to certain products? If you don't want certain products on your hair, don't be afraid to tell the hairdresser.

Don't put on any . . . please
No me ponga . . . por favor
noh meh pohn-gah . . . pohr favor

Product	Spanish	Pronunciation
conditioner	suavisante	swah-bee-sahn-teh
gel	gomina, gelatina	goh-mee-nah, geh-lah-tee-nah
hair spray	laca	lah-kah
lotion	loción	loh-see-yohn
mousse	espuma	lah ehs-poo-mah
shampoo	champú	chahm-poo

Don't forget to ask about tipping:

> Is the tip included?
> ¿Está incluidá la propina?
> ehs-tah een-kloo-wee-doh lah proh-pee-nah

Problems in General

The following phrases will come in handy when you are seeking certain services or are trying to have something repaired. Use them at the dry cleaner, the shoemaker, the optician, the jeweler, or the camera store.

At what time do you open?
¿A qué hora abre Ud?
ah keh oh-rah ah-breh oo-sted

At what time do you close?
¿A qué hora cierra Ud?
ah keh oh-rah see-yeh-rah oo-stehd

What days are you open? closed?
¿Qué días está Ud. abierto? cerrado?
keh dee-yahs ehs-tah oo-stehd ah-bee-yehr-toh?
seh-rah-doh

Can you fix it (them) today?
¿Puede Ud. arreglarmelo (la, los, las) hoy?
pweh-deh oo-stehd ah-rreh-glahr-meh-loh
(lah, lohs, lahs) oy

Can you fix it (them) temporarily (while I wait)?
¿Puede Ud. arreglarmelo (la, los, las) temporalmente
(mientras yo espero)?
pweh-deh oo-stehd ah-rreh-glahr-meh-loh (lah, lohs,
lahs) tehm-poh-rahl-mehn-teh (mee-yehn-trahs yoh
ehs-peh-roh)

How long do I have to wait?
¿Cuánto tiempo tengo que esperar?
kwahn-toh tee-yehm-poh tehn-goh keh ehs-peh-rahr

How much do I owe you?
¿Cuánto le debo?
kwahn-toh leh deh-boh

Do you accept credit cards (traveler's checks)?
¿Acepta tarjetas de crédito (cheques de viajero)?
ahk-sehp-tah tahr-heh-tahs deh kreh-dee-toh
(cheh-kehs deh bee-yah-heh-roh)

May I have a receipt?
¿Me puede dar un recibo?
meh pweh-deh dahr oon rreh-see-boh

At the Dry Cleaner's

You've unpacked. Your white shirt looks like you slept in it, and your beige pants have an ugly stain you hadn't noticed before. Don't fret. Your stains, spots, tears, and wrinkles can be taken care of if you know how to explain your problem and how to ask for the necessary service.

I have a problem.	There is (are) . . .
Tengo un problema.	Hay . . .
teh-goh oon proh-bleh-mah	ahy

Phrase	Spanish	Pronunciation
a hole	un hueco	oon weh-koh
a missing button, missing buttons	un botón perdido, botones perdidos	oon boh-tohn pehr-dee-doh, boh-toh-nehs pehr-dee-dohs
a spot, a stain	una mancha	oo-nah mahn-chah

Now that you've explained the problem, state what you'd like done about it:

Can you (dry) clean this (these) . . . for me?
¿Puede Ud. lavarme este (esta, estos, estas) . . . (en seco)?
pweh-deh oo-steh lah-bahr-meh ehs-teh (ehs-tah, ehs-tohs, ehs-tahs) . . . (ehn seh-koh)

Can you please mend this (these) . . . for me?
¿Puede Ud. remendarme este (esta, estos, estas) . . .?
pweh-deh oo-stehd rreh-mehn-dahr-meh ehs-teh (ehs-tah, ehs-tohs, ehs-tahs)

Can you please press this (these) . . . for me?
¿Puede Ud. plancharme este (esta, estos, estas) . . .?
pweh-deh oo-stehd plahn-chahr-meh ehs-teh (ehs-tah, ehs-tohs, ehs-tahs)

Can you please starch this (these) . . . for me?
¿Puede Ud. almidonarme este (esta, estos, estas) . . .?
pweh-deh oo-stehd ahl-mee-doh-nahr-meh ehs-teh (ehs-tah, ehs-tohs, ehs-tahs)

Can you please weave this (these) . . . for me?
¿Puede Ud. tejerme este (esta, estos, estas . . .?
pweh-deh oo-stehd teh-hehr-meh ehs-teh (ehs-tah, ehs-tohs, ehs-tahs)

Something Extra

If you'd like a service performed for yourself or someone else, use the appropriate indirect object: me (for me), te (for you), le (for him or her), nos (for us), vos (for you), les (for them).

Can you please mend this pair of pants for him (her)?
¿Puede Ud. tejerle este pantalon?

I need it (them) . . .
Lo (la, los, las) necesito . . .
loh (lah, lohs, lahs) neh-seh-see-toh . . .

today.	tomorrow.
hoy.	mañana.
oy	mah-nyah-nah
this afternoon.	the day after tomorrow.
esta tarde.	pasado mañana.
ehs-tah tahr-deh	pah-sah-doh mah-nyah-nah
tonight.	next week.
esta noche.	la semana próxima.
ehs-tah noh-cheh	lah seh-mah-nah prohk-see-mah

At the Laundromat

If your laundry has piled up and you don't mind doing it yourself, you might try to seek out a Laundromat. Use the following phrases to get the information you need:

I'd like to wash my clothes.
Quiero limpiarme la ropa.
kee-yeh-roh leem-pee-yahr-meh lah rroh-pah

I'd like to have my clothes washed.
Quiero que me laven la ropa.
kee-yeh-roh keh meh lah-behn lah rroh-pah

So you're embarrassed to have anyone see your dirty laundry. Or perhaps you're afraid your new silk shirt will get ruined by an amateur. If you want to do the job yourself, the following phrases might serve you well:

Is there a free washing machine (dryer)?
¿Hay una máquina de lavar (secadora) libre?
ahy oo-nah mah-kee-nah del lah-bahr (seh-kah-doh-rah) lee-breh

Where can I can buy soap powder?
¿Dónde puedo comprar jabón en polvo?
dohn-deh pweh-doh kohm-prahr hah-bohn ehn pohl-boh

I need bleach.
Necesito lejía.
neh-seh-see-toh leh-hee-yah

At the Shoemaker's

Let's say you've walked so much you've worn down the soles of your shoes. Perhaps you've broken a shoelace on your dress shoes or you just want a shine. The following phrases will help you describe your problem:

Can you repair . . . for me?
¿Puede Ud. remendarme . . .?
pweh-deh oo-stehd rreh-mehn-dahr-meh

these shoes	this heel
estos zapatos	este tacón
ehs-tohs sah-pah-tohs	ehs-teh tah-kohn

these boots	this sole
estas botas	esta suela
ehs-tahs boh-tahs	ehs-tah sweh-lah

Do you sell shoe laces?
¿Vende Ud. cordones de zapato?
behn-deh oo-stehd kohr-doh-nehs deh sah-pah-toh

I'd like a shoe shine.
Quiero una limpieza de zapatos
kee-yeh-roh oo-nah leem-pee-yeh-sah deh sah-pah-tohs

When can I have them?
¿Cuándo los tendrá?
kwahn-doh lohs tehn-drah

I need them by Tuesday (without fail).
Los necesito para el martes (sin falta).
lohs neh-seh-see-toh pah-rah ehl mahr-tehs (seen fahl-tah)

At the Optician's

What could be more annoying than losing or tearing a
contact lens or breaking or losing a pair of glasses while
away from home? For people who depend on these optical
necessities, the following phrases could one day prove
useful:

Can you repair these glasses for me?
¿Puede Ud. arreglarme estos lentes (estas gafas)?
pweh-deh oo-stehd ah-rreh-glahr-meh ehs-tohs lehn-
tehs (ehs-tahs gah-fahs)

Can you tighten the screws?
¿Puede apretar los tornillitos?
pweh-deh ah-preh-tahr lohs tohr-neh-yee-tohs

The lens (the frame) is broken.
El lente (la montura) está roto(a).
ehl leh-teh (lah mohn-too-rah) ehs-tah rroh-toh(tah)

I need the glasses as soon as possible.
Necesito las gafas inmediatamente.
neh-seh-see-toh lahs gah-fahs
een-meh-dee-yah-tah-mehn-teh

Can you fix them quickly?
¿Puede repararlas rápidamente?
pweh-deh rreh-pah-rahr-lahs rrah-pee-dah-mehn-teh

Can you replace this contact lens?
¿Puede Ud. darme otra lentilla (otro lente) de contacto?
pweh-deh oo-stehd dahr-meh oh-trah lehn-tee-yah
(oh-troh lehn-teh) deh kohn-tahk-toh

Do you have progressive lenses?
¿Tiene Ud. lentes progresivos?
tee-yeh-neh oo-stehd leh-tehs proh-greh-see-bohs

Do you sell sunglasses?
¿Vende Ud. lentes (gafas) de sol?
behn-deh oo-stehd leh-tehs (gah-gahs) deh sohl

At the Jeweler's

If your watch has stopped or isn't working as it should,
you might find it necessary to have it repaired before re-
turning home.

Can you repair this watch?
¿Puede Ud. arreglarme este reloj?
pweh-deh oo-stehd ah-rreh-glahr-meh ehs-teh rreh-loh?

My watch doesn't work.
Mi reloj no funciona.
mee rreh-loh noh foonk-see-yoh-nah

My watch has stopped.
Mi reloj está parado.
mee rreh-loh ehs-tah pah-rah-doh

My watch is fast (slow).
Mi reloj se adelanta (se atrasa).
mee rreh-loh seh ah-deh-lahn-tah (seh ah-trah-sah)

When will it be ready?
¿Cuándo estará listo?
kwahn-doh ehs-tah-rah lees-toh

Do you sell bands (batteries)?
¿Vende Ud. pulsos (baterías?)
behn-deh oo-stehd pool-sohs (bah-teh-ree-yahs)

At the Camera Shop

For many people, a vacation is not a vacation unless they capture it on film. If you need to visit a camera shop or a film store in a Spanish-speaking country, the following words and phrases will come in handy:

Term	Spanish	Pronunciation
a camera	una cámara	oo-nah kah-mah-rah
film	una película	oo-nah peh-lee-koo-lah
a video camera	una videocámara	oo-nah bee-deh-yoh kah-mah-rah

If you have special needs, you might ask:

Can you fix this camera?
Puede arreglar esta cámara?
pweh-deh ah-rreh-glahr ehs-tah kah-mah-rah

I need a new battery.
Necesito una nueva pila.
neh-seh-see-toh oo-nah nweh-bah pee-lah

How much will the repair cost?
¿Cuánto costará el arreglo?
kwahn-toh kohs-tah-rah ehl ah-rreh-gloh

I need it as soon as possible.
Lo (la) necesito lo más pronto posible.
loh (lah) neh-seh-see-toh loh mahs prohn-toh poh-see-bleh

Do you sell film for slides?
¿Vende Ud. películas para diapositivas?
behn-deh oo-stehd peh-lee-koo-lahs pah-rah
dee-yah-poh-see-tee-bahs

I would like to have this film developed.
Quiero que me revele este carrete (rollo).
kee-yeh-roh keh meh rreh-beh-leh ehs-teh
kah-rreh-teh (rroh-yoh)

Other Services

You also might need special services from time to time.
You might, for example, need to find your consulate to report a lost passport. Or perhaps your handbag has been
stolen and you'd like to file a police report. You might
even want a translator to make sure you don't get into
deeper trouble. The following phrases should help:

Where is . . .
¿Dónde está . . .?
dohn-deh ehs-tah

> the police station?
> la comisaria de policia
> lah koh-mee-sah-ree-yah deh poh-lee-see-yah

> the American consulate?
> el consulado americano
> ehl kohn-soo-lah-doh ah-meh-ree-kah-noh

> the American embassy?
> la embajada americana
> lah ehm-bah-hah-dah ah-meh-ree-kah-nah

I lost . . .
Yo perdí . . .
yoh pehr-dee

> my passport.
> mi pasaporte.
> mee pah-sah-pohr-teh

> my wallet.
> mi cartera.
> mee kahr-teh-rah

Help me, please.
Ayúdeme, por favor.
ah-yoo-deh-meh pohr fah-bohr

I need an interpreter.
Necesito un interprete.
neh-seh-see-toh oon een-tehr-preh-teh

Does anyone here speak English?
¿Hay alguien aquí que hable inglés?
ahy ahl-gee-yehn ah-kee keh ah-bleh een-glehs

Fast Forward

Pretend you are having a problem in a Spanish-speaking
country. Explain what is the matter in Spanish to get help.

Is There a Doctor on Call?

Falling ill when you're away from home is hard enough. The situation becomes even tougher if you can't communicate what's wrong. In this chapter, you will learn how to explain your ailments and how long you've been experiencing the symptoms.

Where Does It Hurt?

When traveling, it pays to be prepared if illness strikes. To begin with, familiarize yourself with the parts of the body in Table 13.1.

Table 13.1 Parts of the Body

Body Part	Spanish	Pronunciation
ankle	el tobillo	ehl toh-bee-yoh
arm	el brazo	ehl brah-soh
back	la espalda	lah ehs-pahl-dah
body	el cuerpo	ehl kwehr-poh
brain	el cerebro	ehl seh-reh-broh
calf	la pantorrilla	lah pahn-toh-rree-yah
cheek	la mejilla	lah meh-hee-yah
chest	el pecho	ehl peh-choh
chin	la barbilla	lah bahr-bee-yah
ear	la oreja	lah oh-reh-hah
elbow	el codo	ehl koh-doh
eye	el ojo	ehl oh-hoh
face	la figura, la cara	lah fee-goo-rah, lah kah-rah
finger	el dedo	ehl deh-doh
foot	el pie	ehl pee-yeh
forehead	la frente	lah frehn-teh
gall bladder	la vejiga de la bilis	lah beh-hee-gah deh lah bee-lees
gland	la glándula	lah glahn-doo-lah
hair	el pelo	ehl peh-loh
hand	la mano	lah mah-noh
head	la cabeza	lah kah-beh-sah
heart	el corazón	ehl koh-rah-sohn
hip	la cadera	lah kah-deh-rah
kidney	el riñon	ehl rree-nyohn
knee	la rodilla	lah rroh-dee-yah
leg	la pierna	lah pee-yehr-nah
lip	el labio	el lah-bee-yoh
liver	el hígado	ehl ee-gah-doh

Body Part	Spanish	Pronunciation
lung	el pulmón	ehl pool-mohn
mouth	la boca	lah boh-kah
nail	la uña	lah oo-nyah
neck	el cuello	ehl kweh-yoh
nose	la nariz	lah nah-rees
skin	la piel	lah pee-yehl
shoulder	el hombro	ehl ohm-broh
spine	la espina	lah ehs-pee-nah
spleen	el bazo	ehl bah-soh
stomach	el estómago	ehl ehs-toh-mah-goh
throat	la garganta	lah gar-gahn-tah
toe	el dedo de pie	ehl deh-doh deh pee-yeh
tongue	la lengua	lah lehn-gwah
tooth	el diente	ehl dee-yehn-teh
waist	el talle	ehl tah-yeh
wrist	la muñeca	lah moo-nyeh-kah

Fast Forward

Take a doll and label the most important body parts. Use small tags and push pins or tape. Place the doll in full view so you can practice the names you feel will be useful to you.

It Hurts Me Right Here

Do you want to avoid a trip to the doctor while on vacation? The best piece of advice anyone can give you is this: If you don't have a cast-iron stomach, don't drink tap water when you travel. Let's say you ignored this warning, however, because you truly believe Montezuma's Revenge (also known as severe diarrhea) is a thing of the past. You ate salad greens washed in tap water. Or you ordered a drink on the rocks, forgetting the future gastrointestinal effects the ice cubes might have. You've spent the better part of a day in el baño (the bathroom), and now you feel you must see a doctor. The obvious first question will be "What's the matter with you?" "¿Qué le pasa?" (keh leh pah-sah) To express what hurts or what bothers you, use the expression tener dolor de (en) + the part of the body.

I have a stomach ache.
Tengo dolor del estómago.
teh-goh doh-lohr dehl ehs-toh-mah-goh

He has a pain in his foot.
Tiene dolor en el pie.
tee-yeh-neh doh-lohr ehn ehl pee-yeh

¡Cuidado!

When you express what is bothering you or someone else, remember to conjugate the verb tener so it agrees with the subject.

Something Extra

Use the following expression if you have to pay a visit to the dentist:

> I have a toothache.
> Tengo dolor de muelas.
> tehn-goh doh-lohr deh mweh-lahs

What Are Your Symptoms?

Let's say your symptoms are more specific than a vague ache or pain. Table 13.2 provides a list of possible symptoms, which will come in handy if you need to describe a problem. Preface your complaint with "Tengo . . ." (tehn-goh, I have . . .).

Table 13.2 Other Symptoms

Symptom	Spanish	Pronunciation
abscess	un absceso	oon ahb-seh-soh
blister	una ampolla	oo-nah ahm-poh-yah
boil	un divieso	oon dee-bee-yeh-soh
broken bone	un hueso roto	oon oo-eh-soh roh-toh
bruise	una contusión	oo-nah kohn-too-see-yohn
bump	una hinchazón	oo-nah een-chah-sohn
burn	una quemadura	oo-nah keh-mah-doo-rah
chills	un escalofrío	oon ehs-kah-loh-free-yoh
cough	un tos	oon tohs
cramps	un calambre	oon kah-lahm-breh

continues

Table 13.2 **Continued**

Symptom	Spanish	Pronunciation
cut	un corte	oon kohr-teh
diarrhea	una diarrea	oo-nah dee-yah-rree-yah
fever	una fiebre	oo-nah fee-yeh-breh
fracture	una fractura	oo-nah frahk-too-rah
indigestion	una indigestión	oo-nah een-dee-hes-tee-yohn
infection	una infeción	oo-nah een-fehk-see-yohn
lump	un bulto	oon bool-toh
migraine	una jaqueca	oo-nah hah-keh-kah
pain	un dolor	oon doh-lohr
rash	una erupción	oo-nah eh-roop-see-yohn
sprain	una torcedura	oo-nah tohr-seh-doo-rah
swelling	una inflamación	oo-nah een-flah-mah-see-yohn
wound	un herido	oon eh-ree-doh

Here are some other phrases that might prove useful when explaining how you're feeling:

I'm coughing.
Toso.
toh-soh

I'm sneezing.
Estornudo.
ehs-tohr-noo-doh

I'm nauseous.
Tengo náuseas.
tehn-goh now-seh-yahs

I'm bleeding.
Estoy sangrando.
ehs-toy sahn-grahn-doh

I can't sleep.
No puedo dormir.
noh pweh-doh dohr-meer

I'm exhausted.
Estoy agotado(a).
ehs-toy ah-goh-tah-doh(dah)

I hurt everywhere.
Me duele todo el cuerpo.
meh dweh-leh toh-doh ehl kwehr-poh

I feel bad.
Me siento mal.
meh see-yehn-toh mahl

I'm dizzy.
Estoy mareado(a).
ehs-toy mah-reh-yah-doh

I feel weak.
Me siento débil.
meh see-yeh-toh deh-beel

Telling It Like It Is

The doctor might have to ask you many personal questions about your general overall health and family history. Be prepared—there also will be forms to complete. The doctor or nurse might ask you if you have some of the symptoms or illnesses listed in Table 13.3.

Have you had . . .?
¿Ha tenido . . .?
hah teh-nee-doh

Do you suffer from . . .?
¿Sufre de . . .?
soo-freh deh

Table 13.3 Other Symptoms and Illnesses

Symptom/Illness	Spanish	Pronunciation
allergic reaction	una reacción alérgica	oo-nah rreh-ahk-see-yohn ah-lehr-hee-kah
angina	la angina	lah ahn-hee-nah
appendicitis	la apendicitis	lah ah-pehn-dee-see-tees
asthma	la asma	lah ahs-mah
breakdown	un colapso	oon koh-lahp-soh
bronchitis	la bronquitis	lah brohn-kee-tees
cancer	el cáncer	ehl kahn-sehr
cold	un resfriado un catarro	oon rrehs-free-yah-doh oon kah-tah-rroh
a chest cold	del pecho	dehl peh-choh
a head cold	el constipado	ehl koh-stee-pah-doh
diabetes	la diabetes	lah dee-yah-bee-tees
dizziness	el vértigo	ehl behr-tee-goh
dysentery	la disentería	lah dee-sehn-teh-ree-yah

continues

Table 13.3 Continued

Symptom/Illness	Spanish	Pronunciation
exhaustion	la fatiga	lah fah-tee-gah
fainting spells	el desmayo	ehl dehs-mah-yoh
flu	la gripe	lah gree-peh
German measles	la rubéola	lah rroo-beh-yoh-lah
gout	la gota	lah goh-tah
hay fever	la fiebre del heno	lah fee-yeh-breh dehl eh-noh
heart attack	un ataque de corazón	oon ah-tah-keh deh koh-rah-sohn
hepatitis	la hepatitis	lah eh-pah-tee-tees
jaundice	la ictericia	lah eek-teh-ree-see-yah
measles	el sarampión	ehl sah-rahm-pee-yohn
mumps	las paperas	lahs pah-peh-rahs
pneumonia	la pulmonía	lah pool-moh-nee-yah
polio	la poliomielitis	lah poh-lee-yoh-mee-yeh-lee-tees
scarlet fever	la escarlatina	lah ehs-kahr-lah-tee-nah
smallpox	la viruela	lah bee-roo-weh-lah
stroke	un ataque del apoplejía	oon ah-tah-keh dehl ah-poh-pleh-hee-yah
sunstroke	una insolación	oo-nah een-soh-lah-see-yohn
tetanus	el tétanos	ehl teh-tah-nohs
tuberculosis	la tuberculosis	lah too-behr-koo-loh-sees
whooping cough	la tos ferina	lah tohs feh-ree-nah

¡Cuidado!

Remember that before masculine, singular nouns the preposition de contracts with el to become del.

Something Extra

In Spanish-speaking countries, medical treatment is covered by the government. People who do not have the means to see private physicians receive care in clínicas. No one is left untreated. People who are more affluent can purchase medical insurance and can consult the doctor of their choice.

Remember to give the doctor any pertinent information that might help him serve you better. You might need some of the following phrases:

I've had this pain since . . .
Tengo este dolor desde . . .
tehn-goh ehs-teh doh-lohr dehs-deh

There's a (no) family history of . . .
(No) hay incidencia de . . . en mi familia.
(noh) ahy een-see-dehn-see-yah deh . . . ehn mee fah-meel-yah

I am (not) allergic to . . .
(No) soy alérgico(a) a . . .
(noh) soy ah-lehr-hee-koh(kah) ah

I had . . . . . . years ago.
Tuve . . . hace . . . años.
too-beh . . . ah-seh . . . ah-nyohs

I'm taking . . .
Tomo . . .
toh-moh

I'm pregnant.
Estoy embarazada.
ehs-toh-ee ehm-bah-rah-sah-dah

Something Extra

Want to know how serious it is? Ask the following:

Is it serious?	Is it contagious?
¿Es serio (grave)?	¿Es contagioso?
ehs seh-ree-yoh (grah-beh)	ehs kohn-tah-hee-yoh-soh

How often must I take this medicine?
¿Cuántas veces al día tengo que tomar esta medicina?
kwahn-tahs beh-sehs ahl dee-yah tehn-goh keh toh-mahr ehs-tah meh-dee-see-nah

How long do I have to stay in bed?
¿Cuánto tiempo tengo que quedarme en cama?
kwahn-toh tee-yehm-poh tehn-goh keh keh-dahr-meh ehn kah-mah

May I please have a receipt for my medical insurance?
¿Puede darme una quita para mi seguro médico?
pweh-deh dahr-meh oo-nah kee-tah pah-rah mee seh-goo-roh meh-dee-koh

Explanations

You might find it necessary to explain how something happened.

I fell.	I cut myself.	I burned myself.
Me cayó.	Me corté.	Me quemé.
meh kah-yoh	meh kohr-teh	meh keh-meh

How Long Has This Been Going on?

Your doctor will probably ask how long you've been experiencing your symptoms. Table 13.4 shows the two ways you might hear the question posed and shows how to answer each question.

Table 13.4 How Long Have Your Symptoms Lasted?

Question	Answer
¿Cuánto tiempo hace que + present tense of verb . . .? kwahn-toh tee-yehm-poh ah-seh keh	Hace + time + que + present tense of the verb ah-she . . . keh
¿Desde cuándo . . . + present tense of verb? dehs-deh kwahn-doh	present tense of verb + desde hace + time
(For) How long have you been suffering? ¿Cuánto tiempo hace que Ud. sufre? kwahn-toh tee-yehm-poh ah-seh keh oo-stehd soo-freh	(I've been suffering) For two days. Hace dos días (que sufro). ah-seh dohs dee-yahs (keh soo-froh)
(For) How long have you been suffering? ¿Desde cuándo sufre Ud.? dehs-deh kwahn-doh soo-freh oo-stehd	(I've been suffering) Since yesterday. (Sufro) Desde hace ayer. (soo-froh) dehs-deh ah-seh ah-yehr

Fast Forward

Practice having an imaginary conversation with a doctor.
Describe how you feel, your symptoms, and how long
you've felt this way.

At the Pharmacy

In general, when traveling outside the United States, you
should not expect to find a pharmacy that carries the
wide range of supplies found in many of our drug stores:
stationery, cards, cosmetics, candy, and household items.
In the Spanish-speaking world, pharmacies are specifically
health related. They often dispense medicines and drugs
over the counter that would require a prescription in the
States. It is not unusual for someone who is ill to consult
his pharmacist for proper medication. Only if the person
is seriously ill is he referred to a doctor. Many large cities
and towns have at least one all-night pharmacy called una
farmacia de guardia (oo-nah fahr-mah-see-yah deh gwahr-
dee-yah). If a drug store is closed, look on the door for a
sign listing the nearest stores that are open.

If you are looking to restock your make-up kit or if you
need a bottle of your favorite scent, you must go to una
perfumería (oo-nah pehr-foo-meh-ree-yah), which specializes in toiletries.

If you are trying to find the closest drug store, you might
want to ask:

Where's the nearest (all-night) pharmacy?
¿Dónde está la farmacia (de guardia) más cercana?
dohn-deh ehs-tah lah fahr-mah-see-yah (deh
gwahr-dee-yah) mahs sehr-kah-nah

When you speak to the druggist, you would say:

I need medication.
Necesito medicina.
neh-seh-see-toh meh-dee-see-nah

Could you please fill this prescription (immediately)?
¿Podría Ud. ejecutar esta receta (en seguida)?
poh-dree-yah oo-stehd eh-heh-koo-tahr ehs-tah
rreh-seh-tah (ehn seh-gee-dah)

How long will it take?
¿Cuánto tiempo tardará?
kwahn-toh tee-yehm-poh tahr-dah-rah

When you're simply looking for something over-the-counter, Table 13.5 will help you find it in the farmacia, the perfumería, or even the supermercado. Tell the clerk "Busco . . ." (boos-koh, I'm looking for . . .) or "Necesito . . ." (neh-seh-see-toh, I need).

Table 13.5   Drugstore Items

Item	Spanish	Pronunciation
For Men and Women		
adhesive bandage	el esparadrapo	ehl ehs-pah-rah-drah-poh
alcohol	el alcohol	ehl ahl-koh-ohl
antacid	un antiácido	oon ahn-tee-ah-see-doh
antihistamine	un antistamínico	oon ahn-tee-stah-mee-nee-koh
antiseptic	un antiséptico	oon ahn-tee-sehp-tee-koh
aspirins	las aspirinas	lahs ahs-pee-ree-nahs
bandage	una venda	oo-nah behn-dah
Band-aid	una curita	oo-nah koo-ree-tah
brush	un cepillo	oon seh-pee-yoh
comb	un peine	oon peh-ee-neh

continues

Table 13.5   Continued

Item	Spanish	Pronunciation
compress	la compresa	lah kohm-preh-sah
condoms	los condones	lohs kohn-doh-nehs
cotton (absorbent)	el algodón hidrófilo	ehl ahl-goh-dohn ee-droh-fee-loh
cough drops	las pastillas para la tos	lahs pahs-tee-yahs pah-rah lah tohs
cough syrup	el jarabe para la tos	ehl hah-rah-beh pah-rah lah tohs
deodorant	el desodorante	ehl deh-soh-doh-rahn-teh
depilatory	un depilitorio	oon deh-pee-lee-toh-ree-yoh
dye	un tinte	oon teen-teh
ear drops	las gotas para los oídos	lahs goh-tahs pah-rah lohs oh-ee-dohs
eye drops	las gotas para los ojos	lahs goh-tahs pah-rah lohs oh-hohs
first-aid kit	un botiquín de primeros auxilios	oon boh-tee-keen deh pree-meh-rohs owk-see-lee-yohs
gargle	la gárgara	lah gahr-gah-rah
gauze	la gasa	lah gah-sah
gel	la gomina, la gelatina	lah goh-mee-nah, lah heh-lah-tee-nah
hair spray	la laca	lah lah-kah
heating pad	la almohadilla de califacción	lah ahl-moh-ah-dee-yah deh kah-lee-fahk-see-yohn
ice pack	una bolsa de hielo	oo-nah bohl-sah deh ee-yeh-loh
laxative (mild)	un laxante (ligero)	oon lahk-sahn-teh (lee-heh-roh)
milk of magnesia	la leche de magnesia	lah leh-cheh deh mahg-nee-see-yah
mirror	un espejo	oon ehs-peh-hoh

Item	Spanish	Pronunciation
moisturizer	la crema hidratante	lah kreh-mah ee-drah-tahn-teh
mousse	la espuma	lah ehs-poo-mah
mouthwash	un elixir bucal	oon eh-leek-seer boo-kahl
nail file	una lima	oo-nah lee-mah
nail-clippers	el cortauñas	ehl kohr-tah-oo-nyahs
nose drops	las gotas para la nariz	goh-tahs pah-rah lah nah-rees
pills	las pastillas	lahs pahs-tee-yahs
razor (electric)	la maquinilla de afeitar eléctica	lah mah-kee-nee-yah deh ah-feh-ee-tahr eh-lehk-tree-kah
razor blade	la hoja de afeitar	lah oh-hah deh ah-feh-ee-tahr
safety pin	el seguro, el imperdible	ehl seh-goo-roh, ehl eem-pehr-dee-bleh
scissors	las tijeras	lahs tee-heh-rahs
shampoo (anti-dandruff)	el champú anti-caspa	ehl chahm-poo ahn-tee kahs-pah
shaving cream	la crema de afeitar	lah kreh-mah deh ah-feh-ee-tahr
sleeping pills	las pastillas para dormir	lahs pahs-tee-yahs pah-rah dohr-meer
soap (bar)	el jabón (una pastilla de jabón)	ehl hah-bohn (oo-nah pahs-tee-yah deh hah-bohn)
sponge	una esponja	oo-nah ehs-pohn-hah
suntan lotion	la loción para broncearse	lah loh-see-yohn pah-rah brohn-seh-yahr-seh
talcum powder	los polvos de talco	lohs pohl-bohs deh tahl-koh
thermometer	un termómetro	oon tehr-moh-meh-troh
tissues	los pañuelos de papel	lohs pah-nyoo-weh-lohs deh pah-pehl
toilet paper	el papel higiénico	ehl pah-pehl ee-hee-ehn-nee-koh

continues

Table 13.5 Continued

Item	Spanish	Pronunciation
toothbrush	el cepillo de los dientes	ehl seh-pee-yoh deh lohs dee-yehn-tehs
toothpaste	la pasta dentifrica	lah pahs-tah dehn-tee-free-kah
tweezers	las pinzas	lahs peen-sahs
vitamins	las vitaminas	lahs bee-tah-mee-nahs
water bottle (hot)	una bolsa de agua caliente	oo-nah bohl-sah deh ah-gwah kah-lee-yehn-teh
For Men Only		
after-shave lotion	la loción facial	lah loh-see-yohn fah-see-yahl
cologne	la colonia	lah koh-loh-nee-yah
For Women Only		
blush	el colorete de mejillas	ehl koh-loh-reh-teh deh meh-hee-yahs
bobby pins	los pasadores	lohs pah-sah-doh-rehs
cleansing cream	un demaquillador, la loción, la leche desmaquilladora	oon deh-mah-kee-yah-dohr, lah loh-see-yohn, lah leh-cheh dehs-mah-kee-yah-doh-rah
emery boards	las limas	lahs lee-mahs
eye liner	el lápiz de ojos	ehl lah-pees deh oh-hohs
eyebrow pencil	el lápiz de cejas	ehl lah-pees deh seh-hahs
eye shadow	la sombra de ojos	lah sohm-brah deh oh-hohs
foundation	la crema, la base	lah kreh-mah, lah bah-seh
lipstick	el lápiz, la barra de labios	ehl lah-pees, lah bah-rah deh lah-bee-yohs
makeup	el maquillaje	ehl mah-kee-yah-heh
mascara	el rímel	ehl rree-mehl
nail polish	el esmalte	ehl ehs-mahl-teh
nail polish remover	el quitaesmaltes	ehl kee-tah-ehs-mahl-tehs
perfume	el perfume	ehl pehr-foo-meh

Item	Spanish	Pronunciation
powder	los polvos	lohs pohl-bohs
rouge	el colorete	ehl koh-loh-reh-teh
sanitary napkins	las toallas higiénicas	lahs toh-wah-yahs ee-hee- eh-nee-kahs
tampons	los tampones	lohs tahm-poh-nehs
toilet water	la agua de Colonia	lah ah-gwah deh koh-loh-nee-yah
For Babies		
bottle	un biberón	oon bee-beh-rohn
diapers (disposable)	los pañales (desechables)	lohs pah-nyah-lehs (deh-seh-chah-blehs)
pacifier	un chupete	oon choo-peh-teh

Special Items

A pharmacy that specializes in el alquiler de aparatos médicos (ehl ahl-kee-lehr deh ah-pah-rah-tohs meh-dee-kohs)—the rental of medical appliances—would either sell or have information about the items for the physically challenged featured in Table 13.6.

Where can I get . . .
¿Dónde puedo obtener . . .?
dohn-deh pweh-doh ohb-teh-nehr

Table 13.6   Special Needs

Item	Spanish	Pronunciation
cane	un bastón	oon bahs-tohn
crutches	las muletas	lahs moo-leh-tahs
hearing aid	un aparato para sordos	oon ah-pah-rah-toh pah-rah sohr-dohs

continues

Table 13.6   Continued

Item	Spanish	Pronunciation
seeing-eye dog	un perro para los ciegos	oon peh-rroh pah-rah lohs see-yeh-gohs
walker	un andador	oon ahn-dah-dohr
wheelchair	una silla, un sillón de ruedas	oo-nah see-yah, oon see-yohn deh rroo-eh-dahs

Fast Forward

Put Spanish labels on the drugstore items you stock in your medicine cabinet. Every time you open the cabinet, memorize the name of at least two items you frequently use.

Chapter 14

Business as Usual

In This Chapter

➤ How to make a phone call

➤ Dealing with your mail

➤ Stationery store supplies

➤ Faxes and computers

Conducting business in a foreign country is always a bit of a challenge. It's crucial to understand how to place a phone call, send a letter, buy necessary stationery supplies, and deal with faxes. Being computer literate in any language is probably one of the most important skills you'll need to possess. This chapter will help you deal with all of this.

If you plan to call long distance from a foreign country, whether for business or for pleasure, expect that someone will have to explain how to use the local phone system. It is also likely that the procedures for making local calls will be different from what you are used to back home. You will want to make sure to correctly express the type of call you want to make. Table 14.1 provides you with some options.

Table 14.1 Types of Phone Calls

Type of Call	Spanish	Pronunciation
collect call	la llamada por cobrar, la llamada con cargo	lah yah-mah-dah pohr koh-brahr, lah yah-mah-dah kohn kahr-goh
credit-card call	la llamada con tarjeta de crédito	lah yah-mah-dah kohn tahr-heh-tah deh kreh-dee-toh
local call	la llamada local	lah yah-mah-dah loh-kahl
long-distance call	la llamada de larga distancia	lah yah-mah-dah deh lahr-gah dees-tahn-see-yah
out-of-the-country call	la llamada internacional	lah yah-mah-dah een-tehr-nah-see-yohn-nahl
person-to-person call	la llamada de persona a persona	lah yah-mah-dah deh pehr-soh-nah ah pehr-soh-nah

Something Extra

Public pay phones (cabinas telefónicas, kah-bee-nahs teh-leh-foh-nee-kahs) are located in some post offices, cafés, and stores and are on the streets of larger cities. Many of these phones provide calling instructions in several languages. Some telephone booths provide local service only. Should you desire to call another city or country, you will have to find a cabina with a green stripe across the top that is marked interurbano (een-tehr-oor-bah-noh).

Table 14.2 provides the words to help you understand Spanish directions for placing a phone call.

Table 14.2 How to Make a Phone Call

Action	Spanish	Pronunciation
to call	telefonear, llamar por teléfono	teh-leh-foh-neh-ahr, lah-mahr pohr teh-leh-foh-noh
to call back	volver(ue) a llamar	bohl-behr ah yah-mahr
to dial	marcar	mahr-kahr
to hang up (the receiver)	colgar(ue)	kohl-gahr
to insert the card	introducir la tarjeta	een-troh-doo-seer lah tahr-heh-tah
to know the area code	saber la clave de área	sah-behr lah klah-beh deh ah-reh-yah
to leave a message	dejar un mensaje	de-hahr oon mehn-sah-heh
to make a call	hacer una llamada	ah-sehr oo-nah yah-mah-dah
to pick up (the receiver)	descolgar	dehs-kohl-gahr
to telephone	telefonear	teh-leh-foh-neh-yahr
to wait for the dial tone	esperar el tono, la señal	ehs-peh-rahr ehl toh-noh, lah seh-nyahl

Problems

Are you having trouble reaching your party? The following are some phrases you might say or hear when you are having problems:

What number are you calling?
¿Qué número está Ud. llamando?
keh noo-meh-roh ehs-tah oo-stehd yah-mahn-doh

(I have) You have the wrong number.
(Yo tengo) Ud. tiene un número equivocado.
yoh teh-goh (oo-stehd tee-yeh-neh) oon noo-meh-roh
eh-kee-boh-kah-doh

What's the problem?
¿Cuál es el problema?
kwahl ehs ehl proh-bleh-mah

We got cut off (disconnected).
Se nos cortó la línea.
seh nohs kohr-toh lah lee-neh-yah

Please redial the number.
Remarque Ud. el número, por favor.
rreh-mahr-keh oo-stehd ehl noo-meh-roh pohr fah-bohr

The telephone is out of order.
El telefóno está descompuesto (dañado, fuera de
servicio).
ehl teh-leh-foh-noh ehs-tah dehs-kohm-pwehs-toh
(dah-nyah-doh, fweh-rah deh sehr-bee-see-yoh)

There's a lot of static on the line.
Hay muchos parásitos (mucha estática) en la línea.
ahy moo-chohs pah-rah-see-tohs (moo-chah ehs-tah-
tee-kah) ehn lah lee-neh-yah

Something Extra

In English, when we want to express that someone is going
to do something again, we generally use the prefix re- as
in retry, recall, recycle, and redo. In Spanish, use the
idiomatic expression volver(ue) a + infinitive. The verb
volver (see verb chart on page 188) must be conjugated.

Vuelva a llamar más tarde.
Call back later.

Yo siempre vuelvo a llamar cuando él no está.
I always call back when he's not there.

I'll Write, Instead

It's far more cost effective to send a letter than to place a long-distance call. Table 14.3 provides the vocabulary you need to send your mail.

Table 14.3   Mail and Post Office Terms

Term	Spanish	Pronunciation
address	la dirección	lah dee-rehk-see-yohn
addressee	el destinatario	ehl dehs-tee-nah-tah-ree-yoh
air letter	el correo aéreo	ehl koh-rreh-yoh ah-eh-reh-yoh
envelope	el sobre	ehl soh-breh
letter	la carta	lah kahr-tah
mailbox	el buzón	ehl boo-sohn
package	el paquete	ehl pah-keh-teh
post card	la tarjeta postal	lah tahr-heh-tah pohs-tahl
postage	el franqueo	ehl frahn-keh-yoh
postal code	el código postal	ehl koh-dee-goh pohs-tahl
postal worker	el cartero (la cartera)	ehl kahr-teh-roh (lah kahr-teh-rah)
rate	la tarifa de franqueo	lah tah-ree-fah deh frahn-keh-yoh
sheet of stamps	la hoja de sellos	lah oh-hah deh seh-yohs
stamp	el sello	ehl seh-yoh

If you just need stamps, save time and pick them up at estancos (ehs-tahn-kohs), which are authorized to sell tobacco, stamps, and seals. When you're ready to send a letter or post card home, look for the red and yellow mailboxes.

Getting Service

You've written your letter, folded it, and sealed it in an envelope. All you need to do is find a post office or a mailbox. If you don't know where one is located, simply ask:

> Where is the nearest post office (mailbox)?
> ¿Dónde está el correos (el buzón) más próximo?
> dohn-deh ehs-tah ehl koh-reh-yohs (ehl boo-sohn) mahs prohk-see-moh

Different types of letters and packages require special forms, paperwork, and special postage rates. It is important to know how to ask for the type of service you need.

> What is the postage rate for . . .?
> ¿Cuál es la tarifa de franqueo de . . .?
> kwahl ehs lah tah-ree-fah deh frahn-keh-yoh

Phrase	Spanish	Pronunciation
an insured letter	una carta asegurada	oo-nah kahr-tah ah-seh-goo-rah-dah
a letter to the United States	una carta a los Estados Unidos	oo-nah kahr-tah ah lohs ehs-tah-dohs oo-nee-dohs
an air-mail letter	una carta por correo aérea	oo-nah kahr-tah pohr koh-rreh-yoh ah-ee-ree-yah
a registered letter	una carta certificada	oo-nah kahr-tah sehr-tee-fee-kah-dah
a special-delivery letter	una carta urgente	oo-nah kahr-tah oor-heh-teh

I would like to send this letter (this package) by regular mail (by air mail, special delivery).
Quiero mandar esta carta (este paquete) por correo regular (aéreo, urgente).
kee-yeh-roh mahn-dahr ehs-tah kahr-tah (ehs-teh pah-keh-teh) pohr koh-rreh-yoh rreh-goo-lahr (ah-eh-reh-yoh, oor-gehn-teh)

I would like to send this package C.O.D.
Quiero mandar este paquete contra reembolso.
kee-yeh-roh mahn-dahr ehs-teh pah-keh-teh kohn-trah
rreh-ehm-bohl-soh

How much does this letter (package) weigh?
¿Cuánto pesa esta carta (este paquete)?
kwahn-toh peh-sah ehs-tah kahr-tah (ehs-teh
pah-keh-teh)

When will it arrive?
¿Cuándo llegaré (llegarán)?
kwahn-doh yeh-gah-reh (yeh-gah-rahn)

I Need Supplies

To successfully conduct any type of business, it is necessary to keep certain basic supplies on hand. No doubt,
you'll want to stop at la papelería (lah pah-peh-leh-ree-
yah), the stationery store, to stock up on the business
items listed in Table 14.4. Start by saying:

I would like to buy . . .
Quisiera comprar . . .
kee-see-yeh-rah kohm-prahr

Table 14.4 At the Stationery Store

Supply	Spanish	Pronunciation
ball-point pen	un bolígrafo	oon boh-lee-grah-foh
calculator (solar)	una calculadora (solar)	oo-nah kahl-koo-lah-doh-rah (soh-lahr)
envelopes	unos sobres	oo-nohs soh-brehs
eraser	una goma	oo-nah goh-mah
glue	pegamento	peh-gah-mehn-toh
notebook	un cuaderno	oon kwah-dehr-noh
paper	un papel	oon pah-pehl
paper clips	unos sujetapapeles	oo-nohs soo-heh-tah-pah-peh-lehs

continues

Table 14.4 Continued

Supply	Spanish	Pronunciation
pencils	unos lápices	oo-nohs lah-pee-sehs
pencil sharpener	un sacapuntas	oon sah-kah-poon-tahs
Post-its™	unas notas autoadhesivas desprendibles	oo-nahs noh-tahs ow-toh-ahd-eh-see-bahs dehs-prehn-dee-blehs
ruler	una regla	oo-nah rreh-glah
scotch tape	una cinta adhesiva	oo-nah seen-tah ahd-eh-see-bah
stapler	una grapadora	oo-nah grah-pah-doh-rah
stationery	unos objetos de escritorio	oo-nohs ohb-heh-tohs deh ehs-kree-toh-ree-yoh
string	una cuerda	oo-nah kwehr-dah
wrapping paper	un papel del envoltorio	oon pah-pehl dehl ehn-bol-toh-ree-yoh
writing pad	un bloc	oon blohk

Fast Forward

Write a list in Spanish of all the stationery items you keep in your home office or desk.

Fax It

Let's face it, a fax machine is becoming almost as important as a telephone in many households. When you can transmit and receive messages and information in a matter of seconds or minutes, you can speed up the time it takes to transact business. That translates into extra cash. If you are conducting business in a Spanish-speaking country, it's a must to be fax-literate.

Do you have a fax machine?
¿Tiene Ud. un fax?
tee-yeh-neh oo-stehd oon fahks

What is your fax number?
¿Cuál es su número de fax?
kwahl ehs soo noo-meh-roh deh fahks

I'd like to send a fax.
Quisiera mandar un fax.
kee-see-yeh-rah mahn-dahr oon fahks

Fax it to me.
Enviémelo por fax.
ehn-bee-yeh-meh-loh pohr fahks

I didn't get your fax.
Yo no recibí (Yo no he recibido) su fax.
yoh noh rreh-see-bee (yoh noh eh reh-see-bee-doh) soo
fahks

Did you receive my fax?
¿Recibió (¿Ha recibido) Ud. mi fax?
rreh-see-bee-yoh (ah reh-see-bee-doh) oo-stehd mee
fahks

Your fax is illegible. Please send it again.
Su fax es ilegible. ¿Puede Ud. enviármelo otra vez?
soo fahks ehs ee-leh-hee-bleh pweh-deh oo-stehd ehn-
bee-yahr-meh-loh oh-trah behs

I'm a Computer Geek

Today a computer is an absolute necessity. You must
know enough about the industry standards and programs
for your field of work as well as for the system you are using. The phrases that follow will help you, even if you're
not a computer geek.

What kind of computer do you have?
¿Qué sistema (tipo, género) de computadora tiene Ud.?
keh sees-teh-mah (tee-poh, heh-neh-roh) deh
kohm-poo-tah-doh-rah tee-yeh-neh oo-stehd

What operating system are you using?
¿Qué sistema operador usa Ud. (está Ud. usando)?
keh sees-teh-mah oh-peh-rah-dohr oo-sah oo-stehd
(ehs-tah oo-stehd oo-sahn-doh)

What word-processing program are you using?
¿Qué procesador de textos usa Ud. (está Ud. usando)?
keh proh-seh-sah-dohr deh tehks-tohs oo-sah
oo-stehd (ehs-tah oo-stehd oo-sahn-doh)

What spreadsheet program are you using?
¿Qué hoja de cálculo electrónico usa Ud.
(está Ud. usando)?
keh oh-hah deh kahl-koo-loh eh-lehk-troh-nee-koh
oo-sah oo-stehd (ehs-tah oo-stehd oo-sahn-doh)

What peripherals do you have?
¿Qué periféricos usa Ud. (está Ud. usando)?
keh peh-ree-feh-ree-kohs oo-sah oo-stehd
(ehs-tah oo-stehd oo-sahn-doh)

Are our systems compatible?
¿Son compatibles nuestros sistemas?
sohn kohm-pah-tee-blehs nwehs-trohs
sees-teh-mahs

Something Extra

To say Internet, use the term el internet (ehl een-tehr-neht).

To speak about E-mail, you would use the term el correo
electrónico (ehl koh-rreh-yoh eh-lehk-troh-nee-koh).

Verb Charts

Regular Verbs

-ar Verbs

Example: usar, to use

Gerund: usando

Past participle: usado

Commands: ¡Use Ud.! ¡Usen Uds.! ¡Usemos!

Subj.	Present (do)	Subj.	Present (do)
yo	uso	nos.	usamos
tú	usas	vos.	usáis
él	usa	ellos	usan

-er Verbs

Example: comer, to eat

Gerund: comiendo

Past participle: comido

Commands: ¡Coma Ud.! ¡Coman Uds.! ¡Comamos!

Subj.	Present	Subj.	Present
yo	como	nos.	comemos
tú	comes	vos.	coméis
él	come	ellos	comen

-ir Verbs

Example: vivir, to live

Gerund: viviendo

Past participle: vivido

Commands: ¡Viva Ud.! ¡Vivan Uds.! ¡Vivamos!

Subj.	Present	Subj.	Present
yo	vivo	nos.	vivimos
tú	vives	vos.	vivís
él	vive	ellos	viven

Irregular Verbs

Example: dar, to give

Subj.	Present	Preterite
yo	doy	di
tú	das	diste

Subj.	Present	Preterite
él	da	dio
nos.	damos	dimos
vos.	dáis	disteis
ellos	dan	dieron

Example: decir, to say

Gerund: diciendo

Past participle: dicho

Subj.	Present	Pret.	Future	Cond.
yo	digo	dije	diré	diría
tú	dices	dijiste	dirás	dirías
él	dice	dijó	dirá	diría
nos.	decimos	dijmos	diremos	diríamos
vos.	decís	dijisteis	diréis	diríais
ellos	dicen	dijeron	disrán	dirían

Example: estar, to be

Subj.	Present	Preterite
yo	estoy	estuve
tú	estás	estuviste
él	está	estuvo
nos.	estamos	estuvimos
vos.	estáis	estuvisteis
ellos	están	estuvieron

Example: hacer, to make, to do

Past participle: hecho

Subj.	Present	Pret.	Future	Cond.
yo	hago	hice	haré	haría
tú	haces	hiciste	harás	harías
él	hace	hizo	hará	haría
nos.	hacemos	hicimos	haremos	haríamos
vos.	hacéis	hicisteis	haréis	haríais
ellos	hacen	hicieron	harán	harían

Example: ir, to go

Gerund: yendo

Subj.	Present	Preterite	Imperfect
yo	voy	fui	iba
tú	vas	fuiste	ibas
él	va	fue	iba
nos.	vamos	fuimos	íbamos
vos.	vais	fuisteis	ibais
ellos	van	fueron	iban

Example: poder (o to ue), to be able to, can

Gerund: pudiendo

Subj.	Present	Pret.	Future	Cond.
yo	puedo	pude	podré	podría
tú	puedes	pudiste	podrás	podrías
él	puede	pudo	podrá	podría
nos.	podemos	pudimos	podremos	podríamos

Subj.	Present	Pret.	Future	Cond.
vos.	podéis	pudisteis	podréis	podríais
ellos	pueden	pudieron	podrán	podrían

Example: poner, to put, to place

Past participle: puesto

Subj.	Present	Pret.	Future	Cond.
yo	pongo	puse	pondré	pondría
tú	pones	pusiste	pondrás	pondrías
él	pone	puso	pondrá	pondría
nos.	ponemos	pusimos	pondremos	pondríamos
vos.	ponéis	pusisteis	pondréis	pondríais
ellos	ponen	pusieron	pondrán	pondrían

Example: querer, to want

Subj.	Present	Pret.	Future	Cond.
yo	quiero	quise	querré	querría
tú	quieres	quisiste	querrás	querrías
él	quiere	quiso	querrá	querría
nos.	queremos	quisimos	querremos	querríamos
vos.	queréis	quisisteis	querréis	querríais
ellos	quieren	quisieron	querrán	querrían

Example: saber, to know

Subj.	Present	Pret.	Future	Cond.
yo	sé	supe	sabré	sabría
tú	sabes	supiste	sabrás	sabrías

continues

continued

Subj.	Present	Pret.	Future	Cond.
él	sabe	supo	sabrá	sabría
nos.	sabemos	supimos	sabremos	sabríamos
vos.	sabéis	supisteis	sabréis	sabríais
ellos	saben	supieron	sabrán	sabrían

Example: salir, to go out

Subj.	Present	Future	Cond.
yo	salgo	saldré	saldría
tú	sales	saldrás	saldrías
él	sale	saldrá	saldría
nos.	salemos	saldremos	saldríamos
vos.	saléis	saldréis	saldríais
ellos	salen	saldrán	saldrían

Example: ser, to be

Subj.	Present	Pret.	Imperfect
yo	soy	fui	era
tú	eres	fuiste	eras
él	es	fue	era
nos.	somos	fuimos	éramos
vos.	sois	fuisteis	erais
ellos	son	fueron	eran

Example: tener, to have

Subj.	Present	Pret.	Future	Cond.
yo	tengo	tuve	tendré	tendría
tú	tienes	tuviste	tendrás	tendrías
él	tiene	tuvo	tendrá	tendría
nos.	tenemos	tuvimos	tendremos	tendríamos
vos.	tenéis	tuvisteis	tendréis	tendríais
ellos	tienen	tuvieron	tendrán	tendrían

Example: traer, to bring

Past participle: traído

Subj.	Present	Preterite
yo	traigo	traje
tú	traes	trajiste
él	trae	trajo
nos.	traemos	trajimos
vos.	traéis	trajisteis
ellos	traen	trajeron

Example: venir, to come

Gerund: viniendo

Subj.	Present	Pret.	Future	Cond.
yo	vengo	vine	vendré	vendría
tú	vienes	viniste	vendrás	vendrías
él	viene	vino	vendrá	vendría
nos.	venimos	vinimos	vendremos	vendríamos
vos.	venís	vinisteis	vendréis	vendríais
ellos	vienen	vinieron	vendrán	vendrían

Example: ver, to see

Past participle: visto

Subj.	Present	Preterite	Imperfect
yo	veo	vi	veía
tú	ves	viste	veías
él	ve	vio	veía
nos.	vemos	vimos	veíamos
vos.	veis	visteis	veíais
ellos	ven	vieron	veían

Spanish–English Dictionary

This dictionary follows international alphabetical order. The Spanish letter combination ch and ll are not treated as separate letters; therefore, ch will follow cg instead of being at the end of c, and ll will appear after lk and not at the end of l. Note that ñ is treated as a separate letter and follows n in alphabetical order.

Spanish	Pronunciation	English
a	ah	at, to
abordar	ah-bohr-dahr	to board
abrazar	ah-brah-sahr	to embrace, to hug
abrigo (m.)	ah-bree-goh	overcoat
abril	ah-breel	April
abrir	ah-breer	to open
abuelo (a)	ah-bweh-loh(lah)	grandfather (mother)
aceite (m.)	ah-seh-yee-teh	oil

Spanish	Pronunciation	English
acompañar	ah-kohm-pah-nyahr	to accompany
aconsejable	ah-koh-seh-hah-bleh	advisable
adiós	ah-dee-yohs	good-bye
aduana (f.)	ah-doo-wah-nah	customs
advertir	ahd-behr-teer	to warn
aerolínea (f.)	ah-yeh-roh-lee-neh-yah	airline
aeromozo(a)	ah-yeh-roh-moh-soh(sah)	steward(ess)
agosto	ah-gohs-toh	August
agua (m.)	ah-gwah	water
ahora	ah-oh-rah	now
ahorrar	ah-oh-rrahr	to save
ajo (m.)	ah-hoh	garlic
al	ahl	to the
al centro	ahl sehn-troh	downtown
alegre	ah-leh-greh	happy
Alemania	ah-leh-mah-nee-yah	Germany
alfombra (f.)	ahl-fohm-brah	rug
algodón (m.)	ahl-goh-dohn	cotton
allá	ah-yah	there
almacén (m.)	ahl-mah-sehn	department store
almohada (f.)	ahl-moh-hah-dah	pillow
alquilar	ahl-kee-lahr	to rent
alrededor de	ahl-reh-deh-dohr deh	around
alto	ahl-toh	tall
amarillo	ah-mah-ree-yoh	yellow
anaranjado	ah-nah-rahn-hah-doh	orange
andar	ahn-dahr	to walk
anillo (m.)	ah-nee-yoh	ring

Spanish	Pronunciation	English
antes (de)	ahn-tehs (deh)	before
aprender	ah-prehn-dehr	to learn
aquí	ah-kee	here
árbol	ahr-bohl	tree
arete (m.)	ah-reh-teh	earring
armario (m.)	ahr-mah-ree-yoh	closet, wardrobe
arreglar	ah-rreh-glahr	to adjust, to fix
arroz (m.)	ah-rohs	rice
arroz con leche (m.)	ah-rrohs kohn leh-cheh	rice pudding
asado	ah-sah-doh	baked, roasted
ascensor (m.)	ah-sehn-sohr	elevator
así	ah-see	so, thus
asiento (m.)	ah-see-yehn-toh	seat
aterrizar	ah-teh-rree-sahr	to land
auricular (m.)	ow-ree-koo-lahr	receiver
avión (m.)	ah-bee-yohn	airplane
aviso (m.)	ah-bee-soh	warning
ayer	ah-yehr	yesterday
ayudar	ah-yoo-dahr	to help
azúcar (m.)	ah-soo-kahr	sugar
azul	ah-sool	blue
bajo	bah-hoh	short
banco (m.)	bahn-koh	bank
baño (m.)	bah-nyoh	bathroom
barquillo (m.)	bahr-kee-yoh	cone
bastante	bahs-tahn-teh	enough, quite
basura (f.)	bah-soo-rah	garbage
beber	beh-behr	to drink

Spanish	Pronunciation	English
bien	bee-yehn	well
bienvenido	bee-yehn-beh-nee-doh	welcome
bistec (m.)	bees-tehk	beef steak
bizcocho (m.)	bees-koh-choh	biscuit
blanco	blahn-koh	white
boca (f.)	boh-kah	mouth
boleto (m.)	boh-leh-toh	ticket
bolígrafo (m.)	boh-lee-grah-foh	ball-point pen
bolsa (f.)	pocketbook	bohl-sah
bonito	boh-nee-toh	pretty
botella (f.)	boh-teh-yah	bottle
botón (m.)	boh-tohn	button
brazo (m.)	brah-soh	arm
bueno	bweh-noh	good
buenos días	bweh-nohs dee-yahs	hello
buscar	boos-kahr	to look for
buzón (m.)	boo-sohn	mailbox
caja fuerte (f.)	kah-hah fwehr-teh	safe, safe deposit box
cajero automático (m.)	kah-heh-roh ow-toh-mah-tee-koh	automatic teller machine
cama (f.)	kah-mah	bed
camarero (a)	kah-mah-reh-roh(rah)	waiter(ress)
cambiar	kahm-bee-yahr	to change
cambio de dinero (m.)	kahm-bee-yoh deh dee-neh-roh	money exchange
camisa (f.)	kah-mee-sah	shirt man-tailored
carne (f.)	kahr-neh	meat
carta (f.)	kahr-tah	letter, menu, card

Spanish	Pronunciacion	English
cartera (f.)	kahr-teh-rah	briefcase, wallet
casa (f.)	kah-sah	house
centro comercial (m.)	sehn-troh koh-mehr-see-yahl	mall
cerca (de)	sehr-kah (deh)	near
césped (m.)	sehs-pehd	lawn
chaleco salvavidas (m.)	chah-leh-koh sahl-bah-bee-dahs	life vest
champú (m.) anti-caspa	chahm-poo ahn-tee kahs-pah	shampoo anti-dandruff
ciento	see-yehn-toh	hundred
cinco (m.)	seen-koh	five
cincuenta	seen-kwehn-tah	fifty
cine (m.)	see-neh	movies
cinturón de seguridad (m.)	seen-too-rohn deh seh-goo-ree-dahd	seat belt
claro	klah-roh	light, of course
coche (m.)	koh-cheh	car
collar (m.)	koh-yahr	necklace
comenzar	koh-mehn-sahr	to begin
comer	koh-mehr	to eat
comisaria de policia (f.)	koh-mee-sah-ree-yah deh poh-lee-see-yah	police station
cómo	koh-moh	how
comprar	kohm-prahr	to buy, to purchase
comprender	kohm-prehn-dehr	to understand
con	kohn	with
contestar	kohn-tehs-tahr	to answer
contra	kohn-trah	against
corbata (f.)	kohr-bah-tah	tie

Spanish	Pronunciation	English
creer	kreh-ehr	to believe
cruzar	kroo-sar	to cross
cuál	kwahl	which
cuándo	kwahn-doh	when
cuánto	kwahn-toh	how much, many
cuarenta	kwah-rehn-tah	forty
cuatro	kwah-troh	four
cubierto	koo-bee-yehr-toh	overcast
dar	dahr	to give
de	deh	about, from, of
de nada	deh nah-dah	you're welcome
de nuevo	deh noo-eh-boh	again
debajo de	deh-bah-hoh deh	below, beneath, under
deber + infinitive	deh-behr	to have to + infinitive
decir	deh-seer	to say, to tell
delante de	deh-lahn-teh deh	in front of
demasiado	deh-mah-see-yah-doh	too much
desde	dehs-deh	from, since
desear	deh-seh-yahr	to desire
después (de)	dehs-pwehs (deh)	after
detrás de	deh-trahs deh	behind
día (m.)	dee-yah	day
diciembre	dee-see-yehm-breh	December
diez	dee-yehs	ten
dinero (m.)	dee-neh-roh	currency, money
dirección (f.)	dee-rehk-see-yohn	address
doblar	doh-blahr	to turn

Spanish	Pronunciation	English
doce	doh-seh	twelve
domingo	doh-meen-goh	Sunday
dónde	dohn-deh	where
dos	dohs	two
durante	doo-rahn-teh	during
empleado (m.)	ehm-pleh-yah-doh	employee
en	ehn	in
en seguida	ehn seh-gee-dah	immediately
enero	eh-neh-roh	January
enfermo	ehn-fehr-moh	sick
enfrente de	ehn frehn-teh deh	in front of
entender	ehn-tehn-dehr	to understand
entre	ehn-treh	among, between
enviar	ehn-bee-yahr	to send
escribir	ehs-kree-beer	to write
escuchar	ehs-koo-char	to listen to
esperar	ehs-peh-rahr	to hope, to wait for, to wish
Estados Unidos (m./pl.)	ehs-tah-dohs oo-nee-dohs	United States
estar	ehs-tahr	to be
este (m.)	ehs-teh	East
febrero	feh-breh-roh	February
firmar	feer-mahr	to sign
folleto (m.)	foh-yeh-toh	pamphlet
franqueo (m.)	frahn-keh-yoh	postage
frente a	frehn-teh ah	facing, opposite
fuera de servicio	fweh-rah deh sehr-bee-see-yoh	out of order

Spanish	Pronunciation	English
ganar	gah-nahr	to earn, to win
gaseosa (f.)	gah-seh-yoh-sah	soda
gerente (m.)	heh-rehn-teh	manager
gestión (f.)	hehs-tee-yohn	management
gobernanta (f.)	goh-behr-nahn-tah	maid service
gozar	goh-sahr	to enjoy
grande	grahn-deh	big
guardar	gwahr-dahr	to keep, to watch
guía telefónica (f.)	gee-yah teh-leh-foh-nee-kah	telephone book
gustar	goos-tahr	to like
hablar	hah-blahr	to speak, to talk
hacer	ah-sehr	to do, to make
hacia	ah-see-yah	toward
hasta	ahs-tah	until
helado (m.)	eh-lah-doh	ice cream
hora (f.)	oh-rah	hour, time
hoy	oy	today
huevo	weh-boh	egg
iglesia (f.)	ee-gleh-see-yah	church
impermeable (m.)	eem-pehr-meh-yah-bleh	raincoat
invierno (m.)	een-bee-yehr-noh	winter
ir	eer	to go
jefe (m.)	heh-feh	department head
joven	hoh-behn	young
joya (f.)	hoh-yah	jewel
jueves	hweh-behs	Thursday
julio	hoo-lee-yoh	July

Spanish	Pronunciation	English
junio	hoo-nee-yoh	June
lápiz (m.)	lah-pees	pencil
largo	lahr-goh	long
lavable	lah-bah-bleh	washable
lavandería (f.)	lah-bahn-deh-ree-yah	laundry and dry cleaning service
leche (f.)	leh-cheh	milk
leer	leh-ehr	to read
lejos (de)	leh-hohs (deh)	far (from)
libro (m.)	lee-broh	book
listo	lees-toh	ready
llave (f.)	yah-beh	key
llegar	yeh-gahr	to arrive
lugar (m.)	loo-gahr	place
lunes	loo-nehs	Monday
madre (f.)	mah-dreh	mother
maíz (m.)	mahy-ees	corn
maleta (f.)	mah-leh-tah	suitcase
malo	mah-loh	bad
mandar	mahn-dahr	to order, to send
mano (f.)	mah-noh	hand
manta (f.)	mahn-tah	blanket
mantequilla (f.)	mahn-teh-kee-yah	butter
manzana (f.)	mahn-sah-nah	apple
mañana	mah-nyah-nah	tomorrow, morning
marca (f.)	mahr-kah	brand name
martes	mahr-tehs	Tuesday
marzo	mahr-soh	March

Spanish	Pronunciation	English
más	mahs	more
mayo	mah-yoh	May
medio	meh-dee-yoh	half
mejor	meh-hohr	better
menos	meh-nohs	less
mensaje (m.)	mehn-sah-heh	message
mercado (m.)	mehr-kah-doh	market
mes (m.)	mehs	month
mesa (f.)	meh-sah	table
metro (m.)	meh-troh	subway
mezclar	mehs-klahr	to mix
miércoles	mee-yehr-koh-lehs	Wednesday
mil	meel	thousand
mirar	mee-rahr	to look at, to watch
moneda (f.)	moh-neh-dah	coin
montaña (f.)	mohn-tah-nyah	mountain
montar	mohn-tahr	to go up, to ride
mostrador (m.)	mohs-trah-dohr	counter
mucho	moo-choh	much, many
muebles (m. pl.)	mweh-blehs	furniture
museo (m.)	moo-seh-yoh	museum
muy	mwee	very
nadie	nah-dee-yeh	nobody
naranja (f.)	nah-rahn-hah	orange
negro	neh-groh	black
noche (f.)	noh-cheh	evening
norte (m.)	nohr-teh	North

Spanish	Pronunciation	English
noticias (f./pl.)	noh-tee-see-yahs	news
noventa	noh-behn-tah	ninety
novio(a)	noh-bee-yoh(yah)	boy(girl)friend
noviembre	noh-bee-yehm-breh	November
nueve	nweh-beh	nine
nuevo	nweh-boh	new
ochenta	oh-chen-tah	eighty
ocho	oh-choh	eight
octubre	ohk-too-breh	October
oeste (m.)	oh-ehs-teh	West
oír	oh-eer	to hear
ojo (m.)	oh-hoh	eye
once	ohn-seh	eleven
ordinador (m.)	ohr-dee-nah-dohr	desktop computer
oro (m.)	oh-roh	gold
otoño (m.)	oh-toh-nyoh	autumn
padre (m.)	pah-dreh	father
pagar	pah-gahr	to pay
país (m.)	pahy-ees	country
panadería (f.)	pah-nah-deh-ree-yah	bakery
pantalones (m. pl.)	pahn-tah-loh-nehs	pants
papel (m.)	pah-pehl	paper
para	pah-rah	for
parque (m.)	pahr-keh	park
pasar	pah-sahr	to pass, to spend time
película (f.)	peh-lee-koo-lah	film, movie, roll (film)
pelo (m.)	peh-loh	hair

Spanish	Pronunciation	English
pequeño	peh-keh-nyoh	small
periódico (m.)	peh-ree-oh-dee-koh	newspaper
piso (m.)	pee-soh	floor (story)
pista (f.)	pees-tah	rink, slope, track
poco	poh-koh	little, few
pollo (m.)	poh-yoh	chicken
poner	poh-nehr	to put
por	pohr	along, by, per, through
por favor	pohr fah-bohr	please
por qué	pohr-keh	why
por supuesto	pohr soo-pwehs-toh	of course
precio (m.)	preh-see-yoh	price
preguntar	preh-goon-tahr	to ask
prestar	prehs-tahr	to borrow, to lend
primavera (f.)	pree-mah-beh-rah	spring
primero	pree-meh-roh	first
pronóstico (m.)	proh-nohs-tee-koh	weather forecast
pronto	prohn-toh	soon
próximo	prohk-see-moh	next
puerta (f.)	pwehr-tah	door, gate
qué	keh	what
querer	keh-rehr	to want
quién	kee-yehn	who, whom
quince	keen-seh	fifteen
recibir	rreh-see-beer	to receive
recibo (m.)	rreh-see-boh	receipt
reclamo (m.)	rreh-klah-moh	claim area

Spanish	Pronunciation	English
reclamo de equipage (m.)	rreh-klah-moh deh eh-kee-pah-heh	bagage claim area
reloj (m.)	rreh-loh	clock, watch
revista (f.)	rreh-bees-tah	magazine
rojo	rroh-hoh	red
ropa (f.)	rroh-pah	clothing
rosado	rroh-sah-doh	pink
roto	rroh-toh	broken
rubio	rroo-bee-yoh	blond
sábado	sah-bah-doh	Saturday
sacar	sah-kahr	to take out, to withdraw
sal (f.)	sahl	salt
salida (f.)	sah-lee-dah	departure, exit, gate
salir	sah-leer	to go out, to leave, to deboard, to exit
salsa (f.)	sahl-sah	sauce
saludar	sah-loo-dahr	greet
sastre (m.)	sahs-treh	suit, tailor
seis	seh-yees	six
sello (m.)	seh-yoh	stamp
semana (f.)	seh-mah-nah	week
señor	seh-nyohr	sir
señora	seh-nyoh-rah	Mrs.
señorita	seh-nyoh-ree-tah	Miss
septiembre	sehp-tee-yehm-breh	September
ser	sehr	to be
sesenta	seh-sehn-tah	sixty
setenta	seh-tehn-tah	seventy

Spanish	Pronunciación	English
siempre	see-yehm-preh	always
siete	see-yeh-teh	seven
silla (f.)	see-yah	chair
sin	seen	without
sin duda	seen doo-dah	without a doubt
sitio (m.)	see-tee-yoh	sight
sobre	soh-breh	on, upon
sombrero (m.)	sohm-breh-roh	hat
subir	soo-beer	to climb, to go up
sucursal (f.)	soo-koor-sahl	branch
supermercado (m.)	soo-pehr-mehr-kah-doh	supermarket
sur (m.)	soor	South
tabaquería (f.)	tah-bah-keh-ree-yah	tobacco store
también	tahm-bee-yehn	also, too
tan	tahn	as, so
tarde	tahr-deh	late
tarde (f.)	tahr-deh	afternoon
tarifa	tah-ree-fah	rate
tarjeta (f.)	tahr-heh-tah	card
tasa (f.)	tah-sah	rate
teléfono (m.)	teh-leh-foh-noh	telephone
telenovela (f.)	teh-leh-noh-beh-lah	soap opera
temprano	tehm-prah-noh	early
tener	teh-nehr	to have
tener cuidado	teh-nehr kwee-dah-doh	to be careful
tener éxito	teh-nehr ehk-see-toh	to succeed
tener ganas de	teh-nehr gah-nahs deh	to feel like
tener lugar	teh-nehr loo-gahr	to take place

Spanish	Pronunciation	English
tener prisa	teh-nehr pree-sah	to be in a hurry
tener que + infinitive	teh-nehr keh	to have to + infinitive
tener razón	teh-nehr rrah-sohn	to be right
tener dolor de	teh-nehr oon doh-lohr deh	to have an ache in
tener xx años	teh-nehr ah-nyohs	to be xx years old
tiempo (m.)	tee-yehm-poh	time, weather
tienda (f.)	tee-yehn-dah	store
tienda de regalos (f.)	tee-yehn-dah deh rreh-gah-lohs	gift shop
tienda de ultramarinos (f.)	tee-yehn-dah deh ool-trah-mah-ree-nohs	delicatessen
tirar	tee-rahr	to pull, to shoot
todavía	toh-dah-bee-yah	still, yet
todo	toh-doh	all
tomar	toh-mahr	to take
traer	trahy-ehr	to bring
trece	treh-seh	thirteen
treinta	treh-yeen-tah	thirty
tren (m.)	trehn	train
tres	trehs	three
último	ool-tee-moh	last
uno	oo-noh	one
usar	oo-sahr	to use, wear
valer	bah-lehr	to be worth
veinte	behn-teh	twenty
vender	behn-dehr	to sell
venir	beh-neer	to come
venta (f.)	behn-tah	sale

Spanish	Pronunciation	English
ventana (f.)	behn-tah-nah	window
ventanilla (f.)	behn-tah-nee-yah	window (ticket)
ver	behr	to see
verano (m.)	beh-rah-noh	summer
verde	behr-deh	green
viaje (m.)	bee-yah-heh	trip
viejo	bee-yeh-hoh	old
viernes	bee-yehr-nehs	Friday
vispera (f.)	bees-peh-rah	eve
vivir	bee-beer	to live
volver	bohl-behr	to return
vuelo (m.)	bweh-loh	flight
ya	yah	already
zapato (m.)	sah-pah-toh	shoe

English–Spanish Dictionary

English	Spanish	Pronunciation
able (to be able)	poder	poh-dehr
about	de, a eso de	deh, ah eh-soh deh
above	encima de	ehn-see-mah deh
to accompany	acompañar	ah-kohm-pah-nyahr
ad	anuncio (m.)	ah-noon-see-yoh
address	dirección (f.)	dee-rehk-see-yohn
to adjust	arreglar	ah-rreh-glahr
advisable	aconsejable	ah-koh-seh-hah-bleh
after	después (de)	dehs-pwehs (deh)
afternoon	tarde (f.)	tahr-deh
again	de nuevo	deh noo-weh-boh
against	contra	kohn-trah
ago	hace	ah-seh
to agree with	estar de acuerdo con	ehs-tahr deh ah-kwehr-doh kohn

English	Spanish	Pronunciation
air conditioning	aire acondicionado (m.)	ah-ee-reh ah-kohn-dee-see-yoh-nah-doh
airline	aerolínea (f.)	ah-yeh-roh-lee-neh-yah
airport	aeropuerto (m.)	ah-yeh-roh-pwehr-toh
all	todo	toh-doh
almost	casi	kah-see
already	ya	yah
also	también	tahm-bee-yehn
always	siempre	see-yehm-preh
American consulate	consulado americano (m.)	kohn-soo-lah-doh ah-meh-ree-kah-noh
American embassy	embajada americana (f.)	ehm-bah-hah-dah ah-meh-ree-kah-nah
among	entre	ehn-treh
apple	manzana (f.)	mahn-sah-nah
April	abril	ah-breel
area code	clave de área (f.)	klah-beh deh ah-reh-yah
arm	brazo (m.)	brah-soh
around	alrededor (de)	ahl-reh-deh-dohr (deh)
to arrive	llegar	yeh-gahr
ashtray	cenicero (m.)	seh-nee-seh-roh
to ask	preguntar, pedir	preh-goon-tahr, peh-deer
at	a	ah
August	agosto	ah-gohs-toh
automatic teller machine	cajero automático (m.)	kah-heh-roh ow-toh-mah-tee-koh
bad	malo	mah-loh
bakery	panadería (f.)	pah-nah-deh-ree-yah
ball-point pen	bolígrafo (m.)	boh-lee-grah-foh
band-aid	curita (f.)	koo-ree-tah

English	Spanish	Pronunciation
bank	banco (m.)	bahn-koh
bathing suit	traje de baño (m.)	trah-heh deh bah-nyoh
bathroom	cuarto de baño (m.)	kwahr-toh deh bah-nyoh
bathrooms	baño (m.)	bah-nyoh
to be	estar, ser	ehs-tahr, sehr
beach	playa (f.)	plah-yah
beef	carne de vaca (de res) (f.)	kahr-neh deh bah-kah (deh rehs)
beer	cerveza (f.)	sehr-beh-sah
before	antes (de)	ahn-tehs (deh)
to begin	comenzar	koh-mehn-sahr
behind	detrás (de)	deh-trahs (deh)
bellman	portero (m.)	pohr-teh-roh
below	debajo de	deh-bah-hoh deh
beneath	debajo de	deh-bah-hoh deh
better	mejor	meh-hohr
between	entre	ehn-treh
big	grande	grahn-deh
bill	factura (f.)	fahk-too-rah
black	negro	neh-groh
blanket	manta (f.)	mahn-tah
blouse	blusa (f.)	bloo-sah
blue	azul	ah-sool
to board	abordar	ah-bohr-dahr
book	libro (m.)	lee-broh
bookstore	librería (f.)	lee-breh-ree-yah
booth (phone)	cabina (casilla) telefónica (f.)	kah-bee-nah (kah-see-yah) teh-leh-foh-nee-kah

English	Spanish	Pronunciation
to borrow	prestar	prehs-tahr
bottle	botella (f.)	boh-teh-yah
box	caja (f.)	kah-hah
branch (office)	sucursal (f.)	soo-koor-sahl
brand name	marca (f.)	mahr-kah
bread	pan (m.)	pahn
to bring	traer	trah-ehr
brother	hermano (m.)	ehr-mah-noh
brown	pardo, marrón	pahr-doh, mah-rrohn
bullfight	corrida de toros (f.)	koh-rree-dah deh toh-rohs
bus	autobús (m.)	ow-toh-boos
butcher shop	carnicería (f.)	kahr-nee-seh-ree-yah
butter	mantequilla (f.)	mahn-teh-kee-yah
button	botón (m.)	boh-tohn
to buy	comprar	kohm-prahr
by	por	pohr
calculator (solar)	calculadora solar (f.)	kahl-koo-lah-doh-rah soh-lahr
to call	telefonear, llamar por teléfono	teh-leh-foh-neh-yahr, yah-mahr pohr teh-leh-foh-noh
camera	cámara (f.)	kah-mah-rah
can	lata (f.)	lah-tah
candy	dulces (m./pl.)	dool-sehs
candy store	confitería (f.)	kohn-fee-teh-ree-yah
car	coche (m.), automóvil (m.), carro (m.)	koh-cheh, ow-toh-moh-beel, kah-rroh
cash	dinero (m.)	dee-neh-roh
to cash a check	cobrar un cheque	koh-brahr oon cheh-keh
cashier	cajero (m.)	kah-heh-roh

English	Spanish	Pronunciation
chair	silla (f.)	see-yah
to change	cambiar	kahm-bee-yahr
change (coins)	moneda (f.)	moh-neh-dah
check	cheque (m.)	cheh-keh
checkbook	chequera (f.)	cheh-keh-rah
cheese	queso (m.)	keh-soh
chicken	pollo (m.)	poh-yoh
church	iglesia (f.)	ee-gleh-see-yah
clock	reloj (m.)	rreh-loh
coffee	café (m.)	kah-feh
cold, to be cold (person)	tener frío	teh-nehr free-yoh
cold, to be cold (weather)	hacer frío	ah-sehr free-yoh
to come	venir	beh-neer
computer	computadora (f.)	kohm-poo-tah-doh-rah
cookie	galleta (f.)	gah-yeh-tah
cordless (portable) phone	teléfono inalámbrico (m.)	teh-leh-foh-noh een-ah-lahm-bree-koh
to cost	costar	kohs-tahr
country	campo (m.), país (m.)	kahm-poh, pahy-ees
cup	taza (f.), copa (f.)	tah-sah, koh-pah
customs	aduana (f.)	ah-doo-wah-nah
dark	oscuro	oh-skoo-roh
daughter	hija (f.)	ee-hah
day	día (m.)	dee-yah
decaffeinated	descafeinado	dehs-kah-feh-ee-nah-doh
December	diciembre	dee-see-yehm-breh
to decide	decidir	deh-see-deer

English	Spanish	Pronunciation
to declare	declarar	deh-klah-rahr
delicatessen	tienda de ultramarinos (f.)	tee-yehn-dah deh ool-trah-mah-ree-nohs
to deliver	entregar	ehn-treh-gahr
deodorant	desodorante (m.)	deh-soh-doh-rahn-teh
department store	almacén (m.)	ahl-mah-sehn
departure	salida (f.)	sah-lee-dah
to deposit	depositar, ingresar	deh-poh-see-tahr, een-greh-sahr
to describe	describir	dehs-kree-beer
to desire	desear	deh-seh-yahr
dessert	postre (m.)	pohs-treh
to dial	marcar	mahr-kahr
difficult	difícil	dee-fee-seel
dirty	sucio (m.)	soo-see-yoh
disagreeable	antipático, desagradable	ahn-tee-pah-tee-koh, deh-sah-grah-dah-bleh
discount	descuento (m.), rabaja (f.)	dehs-kwehn-toh, rrah-bah-hah
to do	hacer	ah-sehr
doctor	doctor (m.), médico (m.)	dohk-tohr, meh-dee-koh
door	puerta (f.)	pwehr-tah
downtown	centro (m.)	sehn-troh
dozen	docena (f.)	doh-seh-nah
dress	vestido (m.)	behs-tee-doh
to drink	beber	beh-behr
during	durante	doo-rahn-teh
E-mail	correo electrónico (m.)	koh-rreh-yoh eh-lehk-troh-nee-koh
early	temprano	tehm-prah-noh

English	Spanish	Pronunciation
to earn	ganar	gah-nahr
East	este (m.)	ehs-teh
easy	fácil	fah-seel
to eat	comer	koh-mehr
egg	huevo (m.)	oo-weh-boh
eight	ocho	oh-choh
eighteen	diez y ocho	dee-yehs ee oh-choh
eighty	ochenta	oh-chen-tah
electricity	electricidad (f.)	eh-lehk-tree-see-dahd
elevator	ascensor (m.)	ah-sehn-sohr
eleven	once	ohn-seh
employee	empleado (m.)	ehm-pleh-yah-doh
to end	terminar, concluir	tehr-mee-nahr, kohn-kloo-weer
to enjoy	gozar	goh-sahr
enough	bastante, suficiente	bahs-tahn-teh, soo-fee-see-yehn-teh
entrance	entrada (f.)	ehn-trah-dah
evening	noche (f.)	noh-cheh
exchange rate	tasa (f.) [tipo (m.)] de cambio	tah-sah [tee-poh] deh kahm-bee-yoh
exit	salida (f.)	sah-lee-dah
to explain	explicar	ehks-plee-kahr
facing	frente a	frehn-teh ah
far (from)	lejos (de)	leh-hohs (deh)
father	padre (m.)	pah-dreh
February	febrero	feh-breh-roh
fifteen	quince	keen-seh
fifty	cincuenta	seen-kwehn-tah

English	Spanish	Pronunciation
to find	hallar, encontrar	ah-yahr, ehn-kohn-trahr
first	primero	pree-meh-roh
fish	pescado (m.)	pehs-kah-doh
fish store	pescadería (f.)	pehs-kah-deh-ree-yah
fitness center	gimnasio (m.)	heem-nah-see-yoh
five	cinco (m.)	seen-koh
to fix	arreglar	ah-rreh-glahr
flight	vuelo (m.)	boo-weh-loh
floor (story)	piso (m.)	pee-soh
for	para, por	pah-rah, pohr
forty	cuarenta	kwah-rehn-tah
four	cuatro	kwah-troh
fourteen	catorce	kah-tohr-seh
frequently	frecuentemente	freh-kwehn-teh-mehn-teh
Friday	viernes	bee-yehr-nehs
from	de, desde	deh, dehs-deh
front, in front (of)	delante (de)	deh-lahn-teh (deh)
gasoline	gasolina (f.)	gah-soh-lee-nah
gate	salida (f.), puerta (f.)	sah-lee-dah, pwehr-tah
gift shop	tienda de regalos (f.)	tee-yehn-dah deh rreh-gah-lohs
to give	dar	dahr
glass	vaso (m.)	bah-soh
glove	guante (m.)	gwahn-teh
to go	ir	eer
to go out	salir	sah-leer
good	bueno	bweh-noh
good-bye	adiós	ah-dee-yohs

English	Spanish	Pronunciation
government employee	empleado del gobierno (m.)	ehm-pleh-yah-doh dehl goh-bee-yehr-noh
gray	gris	grees
green	verde	behr-deh
grocery store	abacería (f.)	ah-beh-seh-ree-yah
hair	pelo (m.)	peh-loh
haircut	corte de pelo (m.)	kohr-teh deh peh-loh
ham	jamón (m.)	hah-mohn
hamburger	hamburguesa (f.)	ahm-bohr-geh-sah
hand	mano (f.)	mah-noh
hanger	percha (f.)	pehr-chah
happy	alegre	ah-leh-greh
hat	sombrero (m.)	sohm-breh-roh
to have	tener	teh-nehr
to have an ache (in)	tener un dolor (de)	teh-nehr oon doh-lohr (deh)
to have fun	divertirse *ie	dee-behr-teer-seh
to have to . . .	tener que + infinitive, deber + infinitive	teh-nehr keh, deh-behr
head	cabeza (f.)	kah-beh-sah
to hear	oír	oh-eer
heart	corazón (m.)	koh-rah-sohn
hello	buenos días	bweh-nohs dee-yahs
to help	ayudar	ah-yoo-dahr
here	aquí	ah-kee
holiday	fiesta (f.)	fee-yehs-tah
to hope	esperar	ehs-peh-rahr
hot, to be hot (person)	tener calor	teh-nehr kah-lohr

English	Spanish	Pronunciation
hot, to be hot (weather)	hacer calor	ah-sehr kah-lohr
hour	hora (f.)	oh-rah
house	casa (f.)	kah-sah
how	cómo	koh-moh
how much, many	cuánto	kwahn-toh
hundred	ciento	see-yehn-toh
hungry (to be hungry)	tener hambre	teh-nehr ahm-breh
hurry (to be in a hurry)	tener prisa	teh-nehr pree-sah
ice cream	helado (m.)	eh-lah-doh
ice cubes	cubitos de hielo (m./pl.)	koo-bee-tohs deh ee-yeh-loh
immediately	inmediatamente en seguida	een-meh-dee-yah-tah-mehn-teh ehn seh-gee-dah
in	en	ehn
instead of	en lugar de, en vez de	ehn loo-gahr deh, ehn behs deh
jacket	chaqueta (f.), saco (m.)	chah-keh-tah, sah-koh
January	enero	eh-neh-roh
jar	pomo (m.)	poh-moh
jelly	mermelada (f.)	mehr-meh-lah-dah
jewelry store	joyería (f.)	hoh-yeh-ree-yah
to jog	trotar	troh-tahr
juice	jugo (m.)	hoo-goh
July	julio	hoo-lee-yoh
June	junio	hoo-nee-yoh
to keep	guardar	gwahr-dahr
ketchup	salsa de tomate (f.)	sahl-sah deh toh-mah-teh

English	Spanish	Pronunciation
key	llave (f.), tecla (f.)	yah-beh, teh-klah
kitchen	cocina (f.)	koh-see-nah
knife	cuchillo (m.)	koo-chee-yoh
lamb	carne de cordero (f.)	kahr-neh deh kohr-deh-roh
lamp	lámpara (f.)	lahm-pah-rah
to land	aterrizar	ah-teh-rree-sahr
to last	durar	doo-rahr
last	pasado, último	pah-sah-doh, ool-tee-moh
late	tarde	tahr-deh
late in arriving	en retraso	ehn rreh-trah-soh
laundry	lavandería f.	lah-bahn-deh-ree-yah
to learn	aprender	ah-prehn-dehr
leather	cuero (m.)	kweh-roh
leather goods store	marroquinería (f.)	mah-rroh-kee-neh-ree-yah
to leave	dejar, quitar, salir	deh-hahr, kee-tahr, sah-leer
lemon	limón (m.)	lee-mohn
to lend	prestar	prehs-tahr
lens	lente (m.)	lehn-teh
less	menos	meh-nohs
letter	carta (f.)	kahr-tah
light	claro	klah-roh
lighter	encendedor (m.)	ehn-sehn-deh-dohr
to like	gustar	goos-tahr
liquor store	tienda de licores (f.)	tee-yehn-dah deh lee-koh-rehs
to listen to	escuchar	ehs-koo-chahr
little	poco	poh-koh
to live	vivir	bee-beer

English	Spanish	Pronunciation
long	largo	lahr-goh
to look at	mirar	mee-rahr
to look for	buscar	boos-kahr
to lose	perder	pehr-dehr
lucky (to be lucky)	tener suerte	teh-nehr swehr-the
machine	máquina (f.)	mah-kee-nah
magazine	revista (f.)	rreh-bees-tah
maid	criada (f.)	kree-yah-dah
maid service	gobernanta (f.)	goh-behr-nahn-tah
mailbox	buzón (m.)	boo-sohn
to make	hacer	ah-sehr
makeup	maquillaje (m.)	mah-kee-yah-heh
mall	centro comercial (m.)	sehn-troh koh-mehr-see-yahl
management	gestión (f.)	hehs-tee-yohn
manager	gerente (m.)	heh-rehn-teh
March	marzo	mahr-soh
match	fósforo (m.)	fohs-foh-roh
May	mayo	mah-yoh
mayonnaise	mayonesa (f.)	mah-yoh-neh-sah
to mean	significar	seeg-nee-fee-kahr
menu	carta (f.), menú (m.)	kahr-tah, meh-noo
message	mensaje (m.)	mehn-sah-heh
milk	leche (f.)	leh-cheh
mineral water	agua mineral (m.)	ah-gwah mee-neh-rahl
minute	minuto (m.)	mee-noo-toh
mirror	espejo (m.)	ehs-peh-hoh
Monday	lunes	loo-nehs

English	Spanish	Pronunciation
money	dinero (m.)	dee-neh-roh
money exchange	cambio de dinero (m.)	kahm-bee-yoh deh dee-neh-roh
month	mes (m.)	mehs
monument	monumento (m.)	moh-noo-mehn-toh
more	más	mahs
morning	mañana (f.)	mah-nyah-nah
mother	madre (f.)	mah-dreh
mouthwash	elixir bucal (m.)	eh-leek-seer boo-kahl
movie	película (f.)	peh-lee-koo-lah
movies	cine (m.)	see-neh
museum	museo (m.)	moo-seh-yoh
mushroom	champiñon (m.)	chahm-pee-nee-yohn
mustard	mostaza (f.)	mohs-tah-sah
napkin	servilleta (f.)	sehr-bee-yeh-tah
near	cerca (de)	sehr-kah (deh)
necessary	necesario	neh-seh-sah-ree-yoh,
to need	necesitar	neh-seh-see-tahr
new	nuevo	nweh-boh
news	noticias (f./pl.)	noh-tee-see-yahs
newspaper	periódico (m.)	peh-ree-yoh-dee-koh
newstand	quiosco de periódicos (m.)	kee-yohs-koh deh peh-ree-yoh-dee-kohs
next	próximo	prohk-see-moh
next to	al lado de	ahl lah-doh deh
nice	simpático, amable	seem-pah-tee-koh, ah-mah-bleh
nine	nueve	noo-weh-beh
nineteen	diez y nueve	dee-yehs ee noo-weh-beh

English	Spanish	Pronunciation
ninety	noventa	noh-behn-tah
nobody	nadie	nah-dee-yeh
North	norte (m.)	nohr-teh
November	noviembre	noh-bee-yehm-breh
now	ahora	ah-oh-rah
number	número (m.)	noo-meh-roh
O.K.	de acuerdo	deh ah-kwehr-doh
October	octubre	ohk-too-breh
of	de	deh
of course	por supuesto, claro	pohr soo-pwehs-toh, klah-roh
office	oficina (f.)	oh-fee-see-nah
often	a menudo	ah meh-noo-doh
old	viejo	bee-yeh-hoh
on	sobre	soh-breh
one	uno	oo-noh
onion	cebolla (f.)	seh-boh-yah
to open	abrir	ah-breer
opposite	frente a	frehn-teh ah
to order	mandar	mahn-dahr
out of order	fuera de servicio	fweh-rah deh sehr-bee-see-yoh
package	paquete (m.)	pah-keh-teh
pants	pantalones (m. pl.)	pahn-tah-loh-nehs
paper	papel (m.)	pah-pehl
parents	padres (m./pl.)	pah-drehs
park	parque (m.)	pahr-keh
to participate	participar	pahr-tee-see-pahr
passport	pasaporte (m.)	pah-sah-pohr-teh

English	Spanish	Pronunciation
to pay	pagar	pah-gahr
pencil	lápiz (m.)	lah-pees
pepper	pimienta (f.)	pee-mee-yehn-tah
to phone	telefonear	teh-leh-foh-neh-yahr
phone (public)	teléfono público (m.)	teh-leh-foh-noh poo-blee-koh
phone card	tarjeta telefónica (f.)	tahr-heh-tah teh-leh-foh-nee-kah
piece	pedazo (m.)	peh-dah-soh
pill	pastilla (f.)	pahs-tee-yah
pillow	almohada (f.)	ahl-moh-hah-dah
pink	rosado	rroh-sah-doh
place	lugar (m.)	loo-gahr
plane	avión (m.)	ah-bee-yohn
plate	plato (m.)	plah-toh
to play games, sports	jugar	hoo-gahr
please	por favor	pohr fah-bohr
pocketbook	bolsa (f.)	bohl-sah
police officer	agente de policia (m.)	ah-hen-teh deh poh-lee-see-yah
police station	comisaria de policia (f.)	koh-mee-sah-ree-yah deh poh-lee-see-yah
pool	piscina (f.)	pee-see-nah
poor	pobre (f.)	poh-breh
porter	portero (m.)	pohr-teh-roh
postcard	tarjeta postal (f.)	tahr-heh-tah pohs-tahl
postage	franqueo (m.)	frahn-keh-yoh
postal code	código postal (m.)	koh-dee-goh pohs-tahl
potato	papa (f.), patata (f.)	pah-pah, pah-tah-tah

English	Spanish	Pronunciation
pound	quinientos gramos, libra (f.)	kee-nee-yeh-tohs grah-mohs, lee-brah
pretty	bonito	boh-nee-toh
price	precio (m.)	preh-see-yoh
problem	problema (m.)	proh-bleh-mah
to purchase	comprar	kohm-prahr
purple	morado	moh-rah-doh
to put	poner, colocar	poh-nehr, koh-loh-kahr
quickly	rápidamente	rrah-pee-dah-mehn-teh
to read	leer	leh-ehr
receipt	recibo (m.)	rreh-see-boh
to receive	recibir	rreh-see-beer
red	rojo	rroh-hoh
relatives	parientes (m./pl.)	pah-ree-yehn-tehs
to remember	recordar	rreh-kohr-dah
to repair	reparar	rreh-pah-rahr
restaurant	restaurante (m.)	rrehs-tow-rahn-teh
to return	regresar	rreh-greh-sahr
room	cuarto (m.), habitación (f.)	kwahr-toh, ah-bee-tah-see-yohn
safe	caja fuerte (f.)	kah-hah fwehr-teh
sale	venta (f.)	behn-tah
salesperson	vendedor (m.)	behn-deh-dohr
salt	sal (f.)	sahl
salt shaker	salero (m.)	sah-leh-roh
sample	muestra (f.)	mwehs-trah
sandal	sandalia (f.)	sahn-dah-lee-yah
Saturday	sábado	sah-bah-doh
sauce	salsa (f.)	sahl-sah

English	Spanish	Pronunciation
saucer	platillo (m.)	plah-tee-yoh
to say	decir	deh-seer
scissors	tijeras (f./pl.)	tee-heh-rahs
seafood	mariscos (m./pl.)	mah-rees-kohs
seat	asiento (m.)	ah-see-yehn-toh
seat belt	cinturón de seguridad (m.)	seen-too-rohn deh seh-goo-ree-dahd
to see	ver	behr
to sell	vender	behn-dehr
to send	mandar, enviar	mahn-dahr, ehn-bee-yahr
September	septiembre	sehp-tee-yehm-breh
seven	siete	see-yeh-teh
seventeen	diez y siete	dee-yehs ee see-yeh-teh
seventy	setenta	seh-tehn-tah
shampoo anti-dandruff	champú (m.) anti-caspa	chahm-poo ahn-tee kahs-pah
shirt (man's tailored)	camisa (f.)	kah-mee-sah
shoe	zapato (m.)	sah-pah-toh
short	bajo, corto	bah-hoh, kohr-toh
to show	enseñar, mostrar	ehn-sehn-nyahr, mohs-trahr
show	espectáculo (m.)	ehs-pehk-tah-koo-loh
sick	enfermo	ehn-fehr-moh
since	desde	dehs-deh
sister	hermana (f.)	ehr-mah-nah
six	seis	seh-yees
sixteen	diez y seis	dee-yehs ee seh-yees
sixty	sesenta	seh-sehn-tah
skirt	falda (f.)	fahl-dah
slice	trozo (m.)	troh-soh

English	Spanish	Pronunciation
slowly	lentamente	lehn-tah-mehn-teh
small	pequeño	peh-keh-nyoh
to smoke	fumar	foo-mahr
sneakers	tenis (m. pl.)	teh-nees
so	tan	tahn
sock	calcetín (m.)	kahl-seh-teen
soda	gaseosa (f.), soda (f.)	gah-seh-yoh-sah, soh-dah
son	hijo (m.)	ee-hoh
soon	pronto	prohn-toh
sour	cortado	kohr-tah-doh
South	sur (m.)	soor
South America	Sud América (f.), América del Sur (f.)	sood ah-meh-ree-kah, ah-meh-ree-kah dehl soor
Spain	España	ehs-pah-nyah
to speak	hablar	hah-blahr
to spend money	gastar	gahs-tahr
to spend time	pasar	pah-sahr
spicy	picante	pee-kahn-teh
spinach	espinaca (f.)	ehs-pee-nah-kah
spot	mancha (f.)	mahn-chah
spring	primavera (f.)	pree-mah-beh-rah
stadium	estadio (m.)	ehs-tah-dee-yoh
stamp	sello (m.)	seh-yoh
still	todavía	toh-dah-bee-yah
stockings	medias (f. pl.)	meh-dee-yahs
stop-over	escala (f.)	ehs-kah-lah
store	tienda (f.)	tee-yehn-dah
subway	metro (m.)	meh-troh

English	Spanish	Pronunciation
sugar	azúcar (m.)	ah-soo-kahr
suitcase	maleta (f.)	mah-leh-tah
summer	verano (m.)	beh-rah-noh
Sunday	domingo	doh-meen-goh
sunglasses	gafas de sol (f./pl.)	gah-fahs deh sohl
suntan lotion	loción de sol (f.), loción para broncearse (f.)	loh-see-yohn deh sohl, lo-see-yohn pah-rah brohn-seh-yahr-seh
supermarket	supermercado (m.)	soo-pehr-mehr-kah-doh
sweater	suéter (m.)	soo-weh-tehr
sweet	azucarado	ah-soo-kah-rah-doh
swimming pool	piscina (f.)	pee-see-nah
T-shirt	camiseta (f.), playera (f.)	kah-mee-seh-tah, plah-yeh-rah
table	mesa (f.)	meh-sah
to take	tomar	toh-mahr
to take place	tener lugar	teh-nehr loo-gahr
to talk	hablar	hah-blahr
tall	alto	ahl-toh
tax	impuesto (m.)	eem-pwehs-toh
taxi	taxi (m.)	tahk-see
tea	té (m.)	teh
teaspoon	cucharita (f.)	koo-chah-ree-tah
telephone	teléfono (m.)	teh-leh-foh-noh
to telephone	telefonear	teh-leh-foh-neh-yahr
telephone book	guía telefónica (f.)	gee-yah teh-leh-foh-nee-kah
telephone number	número de teléfono (m.)	noo-meh-roh deh teh-leh-foh-noh
television (color)	televisión en color (f.)	teh-leh-bee-see-yohn ehn koh-lohr

English	Spanish	Pronunciation
to tell	decir	deh-seer
ten	diez	dee-yehs
thank you	muchas gracias	moo-chahs grah-see-yahs
theater	teatro (m.)	teh-yah-troh
then	pues	pwehs
there	allá	ah-yah
thirteen	trece	treh-seh
thirty	treinta	treh-een-tah
thousand	mil	meel
three	tres	trehs
throat	garganta (f.)	gar-gahn-tah
through	por	pohr
Thursday	jueves	hoo-weh-behs
ticket	boleto (m.)	boh-leh-toh
time	tiempo (m.), hora (f.)	tee-yehm-poh, oh-rah
time (at what time?)	a qué hora	ah keh oh-rah
time (on time)	a tiempo	ah tee-yem-poh
tip	propina (f.)	proh-pee-nah
tissue	pañuelo de papel (m.)	pah-yoo-weh-loh deh pah-pehl
to	a	ah
tobacco store	tabaquería (f.)	tah-bah-keh-ree-yah
today	hoy	oy
tomato	tomate (m.)	toh-mah-teh
tomorrow	mañana	mah-nyah-nah
too	también	tahm-bee-yehn
too much	demasiado	deh-mah-see-yah-doh
tooth	diente (m.)	dee-yehn-teh

English	Spanish	Pronunciation
toothbrush	cepillo de los dientes (m.)	seh-pee-yoh deh lohs dee-yehn-tehs
toothpaste	pasta dentifrica (f.)	pahs-tah dehn-tee-free-kah
towel	toalla (f.)	toh-wah-yah
train	tren (m.)	trehn
to travel	viajar	bee-yah-hahr
traveler's check	cheque de viajero (m.)	cheh-keh deh bee-yah-heh-roh
trip	viaje (m.)	bee-yah-heh
Tuesday	martes	mahr-tehs
turkey	pavo (m.)	pah-boh
twelve	doce	doh-seh
twenty	veinte	behn-teh
two	dos	dohs
umbrella	paraguas (m.)	pah-rah-gwahs
under	debajo de	deh-bah-hoh deh
to understand	comprender, entender	kohm-prehn-dehr, ehn-tehn-dehr
United States	Estados Unidos (m./pl.)	ehs-tah-dohs oo-nee-dohs
until	hasta	ahs-tah
to use	usar	oo-sahr
vegetable	legumbre (f.)	leh-goom-breh
very	muy	mwee
to visit	visitar	bee-see-tahr
to wait for	esperar	ehs-peh-rahr
wallet	cartera (f.)	kahr-teh-rah
to want	querer	keh-rehr
weather	tiempo (m.), parte meteorológico (m.), pronóstico (m.)	tee-yehm-poh pahr-teh meh-teh-yoh-roh-loh-hee-koh, proh-nohs-tee-koh

English	Spanish	Pronunciation
Wednesday	miércoles	mee-yehr-koh-lehs
week	semana (f.)	seh-mah-nah
welcome (you're welcome)	bienvenido, de nada	bee-yehn-beh-nee-doh, deh nah-dah
well	bien	bee-yehn
West	oeste (m.)	oh-wehs-teh
what	qué	keh
when	cuándo	kwahn-doh
where	dónde	dohn-deh
which	cuál	kwahl
while	rato (m.)	rrah-toh
white	blanco	blahn-koh
who(m)	quién	kee-yehn
why	por qué	pohr-keh
winter	invierno (m.)	een-bee-yehr-noh
without	sin	seen
to work	funcionar, trabajar	foonk-see-yoh-nahr, trah-bah-hahr
to write	escribir	ehs-kree-beer
yellow	amarillo	ah-mah-ree-yoh
yesterday	ayer	ah-yehr
young	joven	hoh-behn

Index

Q